# QUESTIONING FAITH

A Journey through the Bible,
Faith, Hope, Love,
History, Mystery, Myth and Science
to the Goal of Christian Good News

*by Sheila Deeth © 2020*

Copyrights 2020 by the author.

ISBN: 978-1-949600-42-1

Published by Inspired by Faith & Science

First print version, September 2020
First e-version, September 2020

All rights reserved. Except for very brief quotes in reviews, reproduction or utilization of this work in any form, by means now known or hereafter invented, is forbidden without the written permission of the author.

Cover image taken by author on Blackpool Beach, 2019

Extracts from the Authorized Version of the Bible (The King James Bible), the rights in which are vested in the Crown, are reproduced by permission of the Crown's Patentee, Cambridge University Press.

# CONTENTS

DEFINITIONS AND QUALIFICATIONS ................................................. 1
FAITH AND ASTRONOMY: GENESIS ................................................... 4
FAITH AND BIOLOGY: GENESIS CONTINUED ................................. 8
FAITH AND MYTHOLOGY: CREATION ............................................. 14
FAITH AND LEGEND: THE FLOOD .................................................... 21
FAITH AND TRADITION: ABRAHAM, ISAAC AND JACOB ........... 26
FAITH AND MATHEMATICS: NUMBERS ......................................... 33
FAITH AND MAGIC: EXODUS ............................................................. 38
FAITH AND LAW: LEVITICUS ............................................................ 49
FAITH AND WAR: JOSHUA AND JUDGES ....................................... 55
FAITH AND HISTORY: THE RISE OF KINGS ................................... 63
FAITH AND POLITICS: KINGS AND CHRONICLES ....................... 71
FAITH AND MYSTERY: JEREMIAH AND DEUTERONOMY .......... 81
FAITH AND THE SUPERNATURAL: ELIJAH, ELISHA, ISAIAH, DANIEL AND REVELATION .............................................................. 86
FAITH AND PROPHECY: AFTER DANIEL ........................................ 94
FAITH AND CELEBRATION: THE BIRTH OF JESUS ................... 102
FAITH AND HOPE: THE STORY OF JESUS ................................... 107
FAITH AND LOVE: THE STORY OF SALVATION ......................... 114
FAITH AND WORDS: THE STORY OF THE CHURCH ................. 119
FAITH AND SYMBOLS: REVELATION ............................................ 124
CONCLUSIONS ..................................................................................... 133

*With thanks to my Coffee Break friends for all their prayers and encouragement, especially to Joyce for "getting me," to Candace for feedback while walking, and to Ginna for her Godly, wise, and careful reading and advice. Thanks also to my mum, who has always believed I had something to say. And to God, without whom I would have nothing of value, to think, write or say.*

# Definitions and Qualifications

If I'm going to write about faith and science and expect anyone to care, I should really start by giving my qualifications. I've been known to describe myself as a "mongrel Christian mathematician," so I'll start with the mongrel Christian bit, and then move on to mathematics.

I grew up Catholic in England, enjoying all the benefits of a Catholic education. I attended some excellent Catholic schools with very wise Christian teachers, frequently nuns. My father was Catholic and my mother Methodist, so the divisions of Christian traditions were always painfully apparent to me. At an early age, when we were asked to pray for any "non-believing parents" represented in our group, I *almost* prayed for Mum. But I felt God tell me He'd chosen her just as she was, and I mustn't ask to change her. So I didn't, which was good—the nuns, as I learned later, had never expected me to. However, I remained deeply curious about our different traditions.

My grandfather was a Methodist lay-preacher; I loved to read his sermons. My uncle served as President of Gideons' Bible Society in England. My younger brother grew up to be a Catholic priest. And, over the years, I've served in various churches and denominations in various capacities: as a communion minister, prayer-leader, lay-reader, home-group leader, Bible study leader, worship leader, Sunday school teacher, and even ordained elder (Presbyterian USA).

I've worshiped as a Catholic, Methodist, Church of England, Free Evangelical, Presbyterian and Christian Reformed Christian. I'm truly a mongrel, in the best sense of the word. I hope, like those gorgeously delightful, endlessly surprising, and ridiculously healthy mongrel dogs, that I might combine the best of my mixed ancestry into something worth sharing.

At the end of my Catholic education, I went to college, proud to get a place at Cambridge University in England to study mathematics. In my final, post-graduate year, I specialized in mathematical astronomy and cosmology. Prior to that I delighted in a mixture of pure (artistic) and applied (scientific) mathematics. I attended lectures given by such famous professors as Stephen Hawking, Martin Reese and John Polkinghorne; I consider myself both lucky and well-educated. Meanwhile, I became Fisher House (Catholic chaplaincy) representative to my college's branch of CICCU (Cambridge Inter-Collegiate Christian Union—pronounced, most pleasingly, as "kick you"); I was a regular attender at CICCU's Saturday night meetings in Great Saint Mary's Church where I benefited from hearing many world-renowned Christian speakers, making me well-educated in faith as well as science I guess.

One of those Great Saint Mary's speakers—I'm not sure which—caught my attention by reminding his listeners that "Faith is *not* the crutch of the spiritually minded; it's something we all live by, all the time." He asked us, at the start of his talk, to define faith:

- Belief in things unseen;
- Hope for things yet to come;
- Trust in something or someone beyond ourselves.

Then he asked, what about science? It's certainly not true that scientists only believe in what can be seen—we believe in atoms and molecules even though most of us have never seen them. We believe in the scientific method. We believe in the value of equations and approximations.

Equally, no one can claim that scientists lack hope in things to come. After all, it's the hope of learning and knowing more that keeps science alive and keeps our theories growing.

Finally, scientists clearly don't only trust themselves—their work is always built on that of those who went before. No scientific theories start in a vacuum.

The preacher concluded that scientists have faith in the work and qualifications of others, in the consistency and predictability of the fields they study, and in the assumption that things should make sense—an assumption that, in the case of historical Western science, was based on faith in the unchanging nature of the Bible's Judeo-Christian God. A scientist's faith today may or may not be built on faith in a sensible God, but it's built on methods that were built on faith in that God.

Meanwhile, the speaker pointed out that we, as young English adults crowding the benches of Great St. Mary's, all had faith that the Romans once conquered Britain. By faith we believed that the emperor once said, "Veni, vidi, vinci." But what made us believe?

- We trusted the teachers who taught us; trusted their qualifications; trusted the institutions that qualified them.
- We trusted the science; trusted those who recognized Roman remains and dated and analyzed them—this even though, for the most part, we couldn't do those things ourselves.
- We trusted the documentation, but only if we had reason to trust the source. After all, there are plenty of ancient stories about Odysseus and the Sirens, but we don't give the same credence to them as we do tales of Roman conquest.
- We trusted the evidence; in England we drive, every once in a while, on long straight country roads which we *know* were laid originally by the Romans—by contrast, we claim the more rolling English country roads were laid by "rolling English drunkards" in later years.

We all live by faith, the speaker said. If we drive and we haven't studied organic chemistry, if we send letters to parts of the world we've never seen, if we eat without growing (and selectively breeding and fertilizing) our own food, then we live by faith. The important question is not *whether* we have faith; rather it's whether our faith is informed (as in believing the Romans came to Britain), or unquestioningly religious (as in "she runs religiously every morning before breakfast, even if it's snowing").

What sort of faith is asked of us as Christians? Is it okay to question the Bible and seek to learn more, even mining other disciplines to provide us with further knowledge, or should we *religiously* believe what our traditions have told us, even if the world around us is snowing contradictions?

In this book I hope to show, come rain or snow, that God's reign as revealed in the Bible will stand up to whatever the world throws at it. Let them throw. Let them question. Let them see, and let the Bible reveal.

*For more about how the Christian faith and science might interact, read Haarsma and Haarsma's* Origins: A Reformed Look at Creation, Design, and Evolution, *or Gregg Davidson's* Friend of Science, Friend of Faith.

# Faith and Astronomy: Genesis

If Roman Britain gives us an example of secular faith, the study of cosmology can offer a fine example of religious science. The Big Bang debate was just coming to an end at the time I undertook my studies in Cambridge, but I should probably set the scene with some background details before introducing the *religious* controversy it provoked among (not necessarily religious) scientists.

- We all know that different materials burn with different colored flames—just toss some paper on the fire, light a sparkler, or watch the fireworks fly. These different colors can be separated into a sort of barcode that shows exactly what elements are emitting and absorbing light within the flame. Emissions will appear as bright lines at particular frequencies while absorption lines are dark. The *barcodes* of light from stars can be analyzed to determine which gasses make up each particular star.
- Unfortunately the barcodes of stars didn't initially make sense. All the lines, bright and dark, seemed to be shifted toward the red end of the spectrum. It was an unexpected finding, so scientists tried to guess the reason why—it's what scientists do. Their top suggestions?
    - Either all stars except the sun are made up of elements not found here, and all those elements, by some strange coincidence, match our barcodes apart from the detail that they're equally shifted to the red.
    - Or the stars are all moving away from each other, like currants and raisins in a loaf left to rise before baking.

Scientists faced with a conundrum generally seek an answer requiring the fewest external assumptions. This choice defines a theory which they can then test. The simplest theory explaining the red-shifted barcodes of stars was that the universe, like that currant and raisin loaf, must be expanding. However...

- If the universe is expanding, all of it at the same rate, it must once have been smaller, maybe infinitely small, maybe like a black hole. The point where the infinitely small universe suddenly comes into being and starts expanding might be called the Big Bang. And such a *big bang* would have certain consequences which scientists then looked for—background radiation at a particular wavelength, certain densities of dark matter, etc. As they found more evidence corroborating their theory, the Big Bang theory became more commonly accepted.

A small group of scientists were religiously convinced that a universe with a *beginning* implied the existence of a *begin-er*, and hence of God. Clinging to this belief *religiously* and refusing to countenance the possibility of God's existence, these scientists refused to acknowledge any evidence for the Big Bang either. Instead of looking for the simplest explanation of scientific observations, this group looked for ever more complicated explanations to get around what was seen. They developed what came to be called the Steady State theory, where space expands because matter is continuously created (by nature, not by God).

Over time, their arguments became ever more tortuous and unconvincing. Meanwhile, over time, the Big Bang theory was refined and gained strength in the light of new discoveries. Eventually a leading scientist in the dissenting group became convinced by the evidence. The Big Bang really happened, he said, and so he accepted God—or at least, some kind of God. We might not recognize this scientist's beliefs—they were radically *not* Judeo-Christian. But I can't help wondering if he invented his own god simply because his Judeo-Christian colleagues failed to encourage him to investigate theirs. If he'd looked more closely at other sciences and compared their results with the Bible, would he have found our God believable after all? If Christians didn't so eagerly decry investigation as *atheistic* science...?

But for now, let's look at that Big Bang from a Christian point of view.

*Genesis 1:3. God begins creation with light, and the Big Bang likewise begins with light!*

Biblical Creation begins, very scientifically, with light. Light on earth? The creation of the sun? Or with the Big Bang? Different readers may have different interpretations, and that's fine. But what comes next? What gets *created* on the second day?

*Genesis 1:6. God didn't just create water; He separated the water out from what was around it.*

While I was studying astronomy and cosmology, scientists were sending space probes to look for water on Venus and Mars. Why water? Because the next prerequisite for life besides light was believed to be free-standing water—i.e. seas on the ground and clouds in the sky, not just water-vapor in a rich pea-soup like the atmosphere on Venus. It's interesting that the Bible doesn't just say God created water; rather, He separated the waters, sky from seas, just like the scientists declared we might need.

Scientists tell us life on earth began in the oceans with plants spreading out onto land. It's interesting, to me at least, that Genesis says plants and trees were the next thing God made—almost as if the tale were being told by an eye-witness—by the only eye-witness to creation perhaps. But then we come to…

*Genesis 1:14-18. If God made light first, why does He wait till now to* make *the sun and moon?*

These verses always confused me when I was a child. Why would God make light at the start, then wait until later to create those things that give light? But now, newly inspired, I found myself thinking about those space probes again. The probe to Venus could measure light in the atmosphere, but the sun, moons and stars were invisible. The atmosphere's too thick and goopy there, just like scientists say the atmosphere on earth would have been until plants cleaned it out! Until the fourth *day* perhaps? That's my interpretation, anyway.

Afterward, of course, fish and birds and dinosaurs (*Genesis 1:21*) would appear on *day* five. Since ancient English didn't have a word for dinosaur, I suspect ancient Hebrew didn't either, but "sea-monster" or "Leviathan" sounds pretty convincing (the King James' Version of the Bible says "whale" since that was the interpreter's translation).Then came mammals, and finally man.

As a scientist, albeit an amateur, I've got to ask how the people writing Genesis, two, three, 4,000 years ago managed to guess the right sequence for everything, even the enormously unlikely appearance of light long before the appearance of the sun. It seems to me the simplest explanation is that somebody told them; and *that someone*, the one and only eye-witness to creation, must surely have been God. (Of course, it may have been a future time-traveler going back to the beginning, but that scenario requires a few more external assumptions and feels less scientific.) So my science strengthens my faith.

My science, of course, may be way out of date. Perhaps there are different ways now to interpret *Genesis 1* and agree with *Science 101*. And perhaps there are other students, all around the world, delighting as I did to find their science strengthening and deepening their faith in different ways. Lots of Christians delight in science (Gregg Davidson, Sy Garte, Frank Collins, and John Polkinghorne for example). But lots of other Christians religiously oppose science, arguing just as fiercely as that Steady State scientist once argued against the Big Bang. Perhaps we can agree to disagree. But we might want to be wary of persuading potential new Christians that they have to *create* their own God because ours is antithetical to science.

> *You can read about the Big Bang debate and discoveries in cosmology (plus much much more) in Stephen Hawking's* Brief History of Time.

# Faith and Biology: Genesis continued

Some Christians claim we can calculate the age of the earth from the Bible's recorded ages of its peoples, adding six days, of course, to allow for creation. Others acknowledge the *days* of creation may actually have been *ages*, allowing for ancient Hebrew's lack of vocabulary words. They might still insist though, that each species was created, fully formed on its right *day*, with no room for evolution; or they'll accept (and define) *micro-evolution* while denying the possibility of change on a macroscopic scale, without recognizing the one might imply the other. All these vocal Christians fuel the science vs. faith debate, claiming that science and evolution are inherently atheistic, reminding non-Christian scientists that there is no hope, and promising condemnation to their children if they should *fall* into believing science. They are Christians, but many, many other Christians fervently disagree.

My understanding of evolution is probably out of date, just like my understanding of cosmology—the science moves so fast. Today scientists study how dormant genes might be activated by the environment. They see new processes at work besides Darwin's random mutation, and it's exciting—God created an exciting world! I read new theories (in simplified form) with delight, while anti-evolution friends recoil from me in horror. Why do they find these studies so antithetical to their faith?

At its simplest, evolution is the result of genetic mutation, and mutations happen, verifiably, all the time. Any mutation can be helpful, neutral or harmful to a species. Harmful mutations tend not to spread—the offspring may die or be sterile. But helpful mutations, not surprisingly, are rather likely to spread. And neutral mutations create the variations around us. We see examples of bird species mutating to fill ecological niches in isolated communities. After a while, birds of one branch won't mate with birds of another—it's hard for a 3-foot bird to mate with a 3-inch relative. Eventually, statistically speaking, a mutation will arise that's beneficial to one branch and fatal to the other. If this mutation spreads in the 3-inch birds, it will make them genetically incompatible with their 3-foot relatives; a new species is formed with no new micro- or macro-method involved in the process—it's just evolution.

And it's just a simplification. As with all science, the theory of evolution continues to change and grow, not because it's "only a theory" and therefore wrong, but because it's a scientific theory and therefore subject to scientific conjecture, hypothesis, and refinement in the light of new evidence.

The evidence for evolution is far more impressive now than when I studied the subject in high school. For example...

- **SIMILARITIES** between creatures lead us to believe they might have a common evolutionary ancestor:
    - Some argue that similarities *prove* creatures were designed by the same creator, each individually, but each with the imprint of the same *artist's hand*. They might be right. But Darwin and others suggested the creator's designs might change over time—God as gardener perhaps rather than magician. They even made predictions to test their idea—that's how science works.

        If evolution was true, they postulated, remains from the (now extinct) ancestors of closely related creatures would be found in more recent geological strata than remains from the (long extinct) common ancestors of less closely related species.

        - The giraffe and the okapi might be assumed to be close relatives, where one feeds from trees on the African plains and the other lives in the forest. Remains of what could be their common ancestor are found in recent geological strata.
        - The giraffe and the pig, however, would be considered less closely related. Fossils of creatures which could be common ancestors of these are only found in much older strata. The fossils, dated by well-established analysis of geological strata, do seem to support the theory.

- o Today we can analyze DNA to observe genetic differences. The same scientific theory as above predicts that more closely similar creatures will have smaller and more localized differences in their DNA. Again, this is borne out by the evidence.
- o We can even perform statistical analyses on DNA differences to determine when *speciation* would have occurred. For example, we might analyze allele distribution—genetic variation—within a species, and compare it across species lines.
  - If giraffes and okapis are closely related, we'll expect DNA analysis to reveal that they *speciated* recently. Results using different DNA strands give similar speciation dates, verifying both theory and method.
  - Meanwhile, tests on the DNA of giraffes and pigs reveal a much earlier speciation date, and agree with the results of the fossil record.
- **DIFFERENCES** between creatures can also support the theory of evolution.
  - o Evolution predicts some parts of DNA will cease to be useful, but still be present, when one species evolves into another. The predicted *junk DNA* is now well documented (though sometimes it's a lot less *junky* than we imagined, which is fun).
  - o Study of differences within a species (different colors of eyes and fur for example) offer clues to how long the defining genes have varied. These results give different *ages* for the *first* member of different species—ages that again confirm the fossil and DNA results.
  - o Evolutionary theory suggests that some beneficial mutations might carry non-beneficial side-effects—a result that would seem natural in an evolutionary theory, but illogical in a theory that insists on individual design.

- A nerve in the neck of a giraffe is found to wind all the way down to the shoulder and back to the head—very strange from a design point of view, but perfectly logical as a consequence of the neck's gradual (evolutionary) lengthening so that a nerve which once went straight from throat to brain gets caught under the shoulders.
- Insect eyes see a much more pixelated version of the world than mammal eyes, but they might spot movement faster than human beings do. So why don't predator mammals have insect eyes? A designer might insert *the right eye for the job*, but evolution will simply tweak what's already present.

So I *believe in* evolution, not as a consequence of religious faith, but as a consequence of accepting the evidence God has placed in creation. Evolution excites and enthralls me. It's like seeing the action of the creator's hand. My *faith in* science—cosmology, geology, biology—together with the opportunity to question Genesis, have left me more convinced than ever that the Bible is God's word.

For me at least, science and faith cannot be enemies. Science strengthens my faith. Faith (and my delight in God) makes me long to know more, leading me to study science. Just like those early Western scientists, who developed the *scientific method* of hypothesis and experiment, I share a belief in God's faithfulness—that He is truly "same yesterday and today and for ever" (*Hebrews 13:8*). Because God does not change, I believe the world God made will obey the same rules yesterday today and forever. So it's worth making hypotheses; valid data can be gathered by experiment; and Western science makes sense.

That said, does it matter if popular Christians in the media disagree with me. Does propagating the belief that faith and science are ancient enemies actually hurt anyone? I think it does.

- History shows such enmity to be a foolish mistake.
    - If we teach the earth must be flat because the Bible says:
        - it has four corners (*Isaiah 11:12, Rev 7:1*) and

- - - everything can be seen from the top of one mountain (*Matthew 4:8*);
  - or if we teach that the sun goes around the earth because the Bible says:
    - the earth doesn't move (various *psalms, 93:1, 96:10, 104:5*) and
    - the sun, in contrast, does move (*Joshua 10:12, Ecclesiastes 1:5*);

  then we risk teaching that our interpretation is more sacred than God's word. Then, like those leaders called out as hypocrites by Jesus (*Matthew 15:9*) we're in danger of "teaching for doctrines the commandments of men."

- The Bible also warns against turning God's children away from him. When we place a barrier between science and faith, we also place a barrier between people of science and faith.
  - We make it hard for scientists, like that former Steady State advocate, to turn toward the Bible. Are we to blame when he creates his own religion?
  - We make it hard for Christian students to remain faithful when they leave home for college. Asked to choose between childhood's faith and adulthood's learning, they may turn from their beliefs, making us the ones who "offend one of these little ones who believe" in God. Do you suppose God has a "millstone" waiting for us? (*Matthew 18:6*)
- Finally, the joy and beauty of our faith can be lost in the argument. If we tell our scientifically minded kids they can love God but mustn't study how God made things work, it's like telling art students they can love Rembrandt but mustn't use new technology to study his technique.

I like Rembrandt's paintings, and I don't know a thing about his style, but that's not the way my brain works. I like Mozart, but I couldn't begin to describe his music; I'm not a musician. But I am scientifically minded. It's the way God made me, and I'm grateful to Him. I love God, and I want to learn everything I can about how He made His world work. God made me scientifically curious. I think God smiles when I exercise that curiosity.

I'm also a writer. God made me verbally curious, and those first verses in Genesis hold the key to a verbal secret that's beautifully satisfying to me:

*Genesis 1:1-3. How did God create?*

I read those words and I ask myself: what's the first active verb, the first action God takes in order to create the universe? According to the Bible, according to every translation I've read, God *said*. He used words. And so this universe, this world all around us, this creation is the *word* of God made manifest, made physical. Meanwhile, the Bible is the word of God rendered into human language. And in *John 1:14* we read, "the Word was made flesh"; Jesus is the Word of God made present to dwell among us.

God spoke three times, and I for one don't believe God contradicts himself. If the Old Testament and New seem to disagree, that's not God changing his mind; it's you and I failing to understand. Likewise if faith and science seem to disagree, I'm convinced the problem's with us and not with Him. My faith is in God, and the Bible is His word. But I'm wary of placing my faith in human interpretations—least of all in my own interpretation!

Are faith and science ancient enemies? I think not. The Bible has no quarrel with science. Faith might lead some of us to interpret Genesis differently, but our interpretations are always and only just that—interpretations. Our *faith* is in God. Meanwhile, science teaches our children to interpret the world God made. Scientific interpretation is always extending the picture, adding, changing, improving, enlightening, because we never know it all. But faith stays bound to one truth behind the picture—God loved; God made; God loves. Let us also love, and not drive anyone away from the God who made us, or from His word.

> *I learned a lot about evolution from Richard Dawkins'* Out of Eden, *though I cannot share his profoundly* religious *antipathy to faith.*
>
> *More recently, I really enjoyed seeing complex science through the eyes of an atheist who became a Christian in Sy Garte's* The Works of His Hands.

# Faith and Mythology: Creation

Of course, not all students go to college to study the physical sciences. Some take classes in psychology, then phone home to ask their parents, "Why do you still believe all that Bible stuff? It's just the cultural myth you grew up with." The cultured student, with the wisdom of new knowledge, proclaims, "You'd believe in something completely different if you'd grown up somewhere else." And so this Christian child, so well-educated and filled with hard-earned understanding—yes, and well-learned faith—rejects the *cultural myths* of his youth and never looks at his Bible again. Rejection, this time, is caused not by the investigations of science, but by the interpretations of mythology.

Which leads me to ask, does the Bible really read like a myth? What if our student children had already tested its stories before they left home? What if *we* could test them too, trusting, by faith, that God will prove bigger than all our doubts (and all of theirs)? Perhaps it's time to find out for ourselves, and teach our children, that the Bible's big enough to stand up without our help.

I've always been a lover of mythology, ever since I learned to read. There was a rather odd rule in my high school; every student had to read two books from the library each week; one of these had to be fiction and the other non-fiction. This caused me much grief, since my school-bag was already overflowing with non-fiction texts for language, science and history classes—why would I want more? For a while I simply rebelled, leaving my unwanted non-fiction selections unread. Then I discovered the shelf labeled *Mythology*. Here was a wealth of wonderful stories, all under the heading *non-fiction*. Here was my chance to beat the system and enjoy myself as well. So, from then on, I proudly selected one fiction and one mythology book each week and devoured them both.

What sort of myths do you suppose I was reading back then?

- Stories of Greek and Roman gods
- Babylonian legends
- Norse sagas
- Native American tales

- Legends of Hindu gods and goddesses, and more… and more.

And I loved them all! I still do.

I overheard an interesting online conversation with a Hindu friend recently. Someone asked how she could believe in so many gods and goddesses with such amazing tales. In answer, she explained that she believes there's only one god, just the same as her questioners do. She believes this god is so far above and beyond our human comprehension, we can only hope to understand and relate to god through the medium of stories—through parables—through myth. I don't know if this e-friend's views are a valid representation of Hindu belief, but I did leave the conversation acknowledging that I don't and cannot know what other people have faith in, and I shouldn't be so quick to judge. Instead, perhaps I should apply more thought and judgement to knowing what *I* believe.

Which led me to think of those Christian *myths* we've adopted to go along with our well-founded Biblical beliefs.

- *Matthew 2:1-12* Were there really three kings at the stable at Christ's birth, or just an unspecified number of wise men visiting the home—maybe even the *house*—of Mary and Joseph and the little boy Jesus?
- *Luke 2:1-7* Was Jesus really born in a dank, dark stable, or in the comfortable stable area of a house of hospitable relatives? I've heard Messianic Jews suggest the dirty stable story is offensive. If all the inns and houses were full, a guest would be invited to stay in the stable of a relative's home—rather like asking them to stay in a garage, with no wall between it and the house.
- *Romans 16:1-7* Did Paul really not respect women, even though he frequently mentions them as having authority?

Perhaps some parts of our religious *knowledge* sound like myths for a very simple reason—that's exactly what they are, based on misinterpretation (maybe *myth-interpretation*) of Biblical truth.

But myths are important, and cultures do indeed cling to their myths, just as we Christians cling to our (mostly Jewish) Bible. That doesn't mean, though, that we can't question our culture. Indeed, if we're to answer the student who complains "it's just your cultural myth," perhaps we need to start *by* questioning our culture; maybe allow the student to question our *myths* with us. Then, together, we might learn the facts that back our *stories* up, and find our Bible stories really are different from the world's mythology.

I've read that all cultures share a *basic human need* to *make sense* of things. It's something we frequently do through story (indeed, as my Hindu e-friend suggested), through myths and the Bible perhaps. I suspect C.S. Lewis might call this an example of our *God-shaped hole*. Then he would remind us that in God, the stories we tell are true and make sense. So let's look at some common (as in commonly found) myths:

- **CREATION MYTHS** try to answer the question; how did we get here? There's got to be a story about that.
- **FLOOD MYTHS** try to make sense of the natural disasters and earth-shattering changes that happen in every civilization. It's human nature to desire that they shouldn't be pointless.
- **HERO MYTHS** provide stories (and heroes) to give us hope in the face of our powerlessness. And finally
- **GOD AS MAN** myths answer our need to feel that we matter. As Christians, of course, we meet the ultimate God-as-man in Jesus.

What makes us (some of us, anyway) so sure that our Christian faith is not a myth, that our answers to these myth-building questions are real? How do we reply when friends accuse us of believing the naïve fairytales of childhood instead of growing up? Do we…

- …remind them that lots of people believe and convert to Christianity? *Yes, but they convert* from *it too*;
- …say the Bible's proved to be true because Christianity spread around the world? *Indeed, but Islam is spreading quite effectively*;
- …repeat that Jesus is a real historical person? *But that doesn't prove he's God*;
- …witness that we know in our hearts that the Bible is true? *But our non-Christian neighbors have hearts too, and are just as convinced it's not*;
- …claim that the stories don't sound like myths? *But other people's stories may not sound like myths to them either*.

Personally, as someone who has long loved myths, I *don't* think Bible stories sound like myths. They're too boring! But that begs the question, what makes something *sound like* a myth? Children might help us answer that one from their own favorite stories:

- The presence of unbelievable monsters: *But there are god-like people, the Nephilim, and giants in the Bible. Read Genesis 6:4, Numbers 13:33, 1 Samuel 17:4, 2 Samuel 21:19…*
- Creatures and people who appear fantastical: *Like Samson carrying his strength in his hair perhaps? Read Judges 16.*
- People with superhuman powers: *But we claim Christ is divine. Is that so different from the Romans claiming emperors became divine as a reward for obedience?*
- Things that can't be explained by science: *But this might require we investigate the Bible* with *science, to prove it's not a myth.*

When someone relates a story to you, what method do you use to tell the difference between myth, fictional account, and something true? In our super-technological world, can you recognize *internet myths* when you see them? Are you sure? For example:

Did you read the story of the girl who goes to the store to buy a miracle for her brother? Her family can't afford medical insurance, but, by divine coincidence, the girl meets a neurosurgeon with the skills to save the little boy. I've seen this one many times—on email, on Facebook, etc.—yet it's known to be an internet myth—a myth that favors Christianity! How might someone know to call it myth?

- Is it proveably false? *Maybe so, but how will that make it different from any other kind of fiction?*
- Is it deceptively false? *Not that anyone expects us to believe in the gods of Mount Olympus these days, but myths are usually meant to be believed in their time. The friends who click* forward *on the story of the neurosurgeon are presenting it as true, accepting and propagating its deception.*
- Is it simply too convenient? Too unlikely? *The girl might indeed meet a neurosurgeon. But a real neurosurgeon would be well aware that finances are just one of many reasons for not doing an operation. It would be cruel and thoughtless to volunteer his help without knowing the whole story.*

- Will it fail to ring true to someone who has the right sort of knowledge? *Yes. Ask a doctor!*

This kind of story seems consistently *less* true the *more* we find out about it. It's not fiction, because it's presented as truth. Yet it's clearly not true. So that leaves myth. But the Bible is *not* this kind of story. The Bible, likewise presented as truth, is filled with stories that seem *more* true the more we delve into them. So let's delve! Let's investigate!

Starting with **CREATION**!

The story of Adam and Eve in the garden (*Genesis 2-3*) sounds pretty mythological on the surface. It may even contradict the account of *Genesis 1*. But the more we learn about early humanity, the more real and human these two people and their children seem. They eat fruit and berries. They walk in a world filled with food. They make up names for the animals surrounding them... Come see with me...

- I imagine Adam's son hearing the story of *Genesis 1*. He wonders if God took so long to get around to making human beings (*Genesis 1:27*) because we were just an afterthought. How would God have answered that doubting child? Could God have told him *no*; before all these things, when "every plant of the field before it was in the earth, and every herb of the field before it grew," (*Genesis 2:5*), we were first in his mind? All this was made for us!
- Meanwhile, Eve pondered if she was somehow inferior, since Adam was the first giver of names to creation (*Genesis 2:19*). Could God have answered her as well? Compared to Adam she was "bone of my bones, and flesh of my flesh" (*Genesis 2:23*) and therefore co-equal with her spouse.
- Then I wonder, was the serpent truly a snake such as those we see in fields, or was it a personification of that slippery voice in our heads—the one that insists on asking, "hath God said," (*Genesis 3:1*) and tempts us astray?

Most mythologies start with creation of course. So here's a quick lay-reader's overview of alternative creation tales. I'm sure I'm missing lots, and oh how I'd love to read them all! But this list does offer a start.

- **World parent myths**: God as father, or two gods as father and mother: *Similarly, the Bible tells us we are all God's children.*
    - Earth and sky are often creation's two parents, or
    - in Chinese mythology, Pangu is born in an egg, which breaks in two to make sky and earth. Then Pangu's body divides to become the different entities on earth.
    - India has the tradition of the golden womb.
    - Native-American tales often include an earth-mother / midwife character.
- **Creation out of nothing / out of chaos**: *This isn't just a Judeo-Christian idea.*
    - In ancient Egypt, the world came out of a lifeless sea of chaos when the first sun arose. The first thing to appear was a pyramid, ascribed to different gods in different versions of the myth. *(Interestingly, the Bible often uses the sea to represent chaos too.)*
    - In Indian stories, the creation hymn sounds very similar to the Bible, one part being translated, "not the non-existent existed, nor did the existent exist…" Existence grows from heat in this story, and desire is the primal seed.
    - Many animist faiths have similar tales of life born from chaos.
- **How the world is built**: *In Genesis 2, the Bible says we are formed out of dust.*
    - In Scandinavian mythology there's a world egg or world tree that builds everything.
    - Many myths have the broken parts of god forming the parts of the world. *Do these prefigure God's sacrificial love in the New Testament?*
- **The importance of names**: *In Genesis 2, Adam gets to name the animals. Meanwhile, in many other cultures, knowing the* true name *of something gives us power over it.*
- **Seven days in a week**: *With English days named for Roman emperors and Norse gods, it's clear the seven-day week is not*

*just a consequence of Genesis 1. Many (but not all) cultures treat seven as a symbolic number with importance in creation.*
- Seven divides the lunar 28-day month into four manageable units.
- There are seven heavenly wanderers, visible to the naked eye, among the stars (sun, moon, Mercury, Venus, Mars, Saturn and Jupiter).
- Then there are seven deadly sins, Snow White's seven dwarves, and seven as the most likely number rolled on two six-sided dice...

*Genesis 1* might seem to tell us the world was made in six *days,* but the earliest languages wouldn't have had words for periods longer than a day. *Genesis 2* might seem to say Adam was the only human, parentless and alone with God, but its words are more in the language of teaching ideas than of teaching facts (plus it contradicts *Genesis 1* if interpreted that way). *Genesis 3* might suggest that nakedness was fine before the Fall but not afterward, but perhaps it represents our nakedness before God. And perhaps...

Perhaps we don't need to argue about whether Adam and Eve were the first created or the first representative humans. Perhaps we'd serve God, our children and our neighbors better by accepting that we don't know. And perhaps our insistence on *knowing it all* blinds us to knowing and showing what we truly know—that the Bible sounds more like the parent *truth* than a *myth* derived from others; that the Bible's six periods (ages or *days*) of creation seem far more scientific than the stories in mythologies; and that the Fall of Adam and Eve prefigures the very same sin that makes us insist on *knowing it all.*

> *If you want to share my love of mythology, you might like to read* Myth and Mythology: Tales from the Ancient World *by Andrew T. Cummings.*

# Faith and Legend: The Flood

I've read lots of myths and legends, and I'm trained, as a scientist, to be a critical reader. I can critically read books of legends and books about them. But I'm not trained to analyze and test legends myself.

That said, I know that experts look for similarities between different stories, then track how tribes and peoples must have travelled the world, by looking at the tales left behind. When they find matching stories in different places, they might deduce one culture *borrowed* from another and built on the tale. Then they'll try to work out which group told the story first. And some of them will question if the Bible builds on Babylonian myths.

It's a question our neighbors and children might quickly echo. But Babylon and the Bible could have happened the other way around: Ancient records of Babylonian myths may be older than ancient texts of the Bible, but that doesn't prove the stories themselves are older. Nomadic herdsmen like the Israelites might not have left written records, or records that survived the floods of time. They might have simply told stories around the fire, sharing those tales in Babylon—embracing them to sustain their identity during captivity, but not creating them *during* captivity. After all, if they were creating new stories for themselves, why would they make them so much less entertaining than the stories of their captors? Because myths really do make for more entertaining reading than the Bible, as I learned during those high school days when I raided the library shelves.

The Bible seemed so boring compared to tales of Zeus and Thor. I began to wonder, *Why didn't God hire better writers?* But I'd missed the point of course. My beloved myths were *re*-tellings, not translations of the original. As language grew richer, each culture's retelling of a story—Noah's ark as a prime example—became more colorful, much as when I now *retell* a Bible tale in my beloved *Five Minute Bible Story Series*.

A storyteller narrates what might have happened, adding details that aren't really there to draw the listener in; encouraging the audience to relate and ask questions, until the story becomes their own; adding twists and turns until the characters come alive.

But what if the Bible's stories belonged to a people who kept their traditions alive with stories *religiously* recited around the campfire? How would their stories sound?

- Like mine, with lots of imagination and details—a story that grows larger with every new telling, or
- like the Bible, with lots of recitation where nobody dares alter "one jot or tittle" (*Matthew 5:18*)?

Which way do you think the ancient Hebrews would have used to pass on their tales? And the ancient Babylonians with their culture of leisure and power…? Hence, I imagine, the relatively *boring* Bible and the vividly exciting chronicles of Gilgamesh, both of which tell of a global flood. (I loved Gilgamesh!)

So, let's look at **FLOOD**s

Flood stories are almost as common as creation myths, perhaps because floods are the archetypal dramatic event that destroys primitive societies. The Bible's story of Noah certainly has many aspects in common with mythology. In its most *traditional* form, it even includes many seriously hard-to-believe details. So, how do we answer someone who says that Noah's ark is a myth? How would you answer these specific complaints?

- There is not and never has been enough water to cover the whole earth. *True, but typically in the Bible, the whole earth means whole of the known earth. The whole of the known earth can and does become flooded.*
- Rain wouldn't cause the water-level to rise so fast. *True, but the Bible doesn't say the rain came first; Genesis 7:11 suggests the floods rose up first, followed by rain coming down.*
- You couldn't fit two of every animal on one ship, or find two of every animal in one location. *True, but you could, and probably would, do everything you could to save breeding pairs of whatever flocks you kept. They would be all the animals you'd care to save or name. The Bible even includes the surprising detail that that ark carried more than two of each food animal— very practical; very sensible even (Genesis 6:19-20, 7:2-3).*

- Rainbows must have existed before the flood. *But the Bible doesn't contradict this. We're not told that God made the first rainbow after the flood. Rather Genesis 9:13 tells us God has set his token in the sky. I imagine God pointing to a rainbow and saying, "Look at that, and remember my promise whenever you see it again."*
- A good God wouldn't kill people. *But, given the fragility of life, perhaps the real miracle is that anyone survived. In Genesis 6:8 we're told that Noah was the only one still listening to God's warnings. If disaster were coming, this would make Noah the only one willing to do what it took to be saved. As far as we can tell, his wife and kids might be as evil as everyone else, but they're saved because of Noah, who is saved because he listens.*

My bored teenage self has grown up to see some surprisingly rich details in the Bible account. After the ark lands, Noah is told not to eat flesh with its blood in it—an invaluable warning, under the circumstances—don't eat flood-kill (*Genesis 9:1-4*)! Then the Bible's first record of drunkenness occurs soon after the landing of the ark (*Genesis 9:20-21*)—it's not impossible that grapes stored in barrels below deck were the first fruit to naturally ferment instead of decaying.

So how does Gilgamesh compare? Just like in Genesis, the Babylonian flood and creation tales are told in the same book. And there are lots of parallels:

- A snake steals a magical plant that can restore health.
- Innocence is associated with nakedness and lost when wisdom is attained. In Gilgamesh, however, that humanly gained wisdom represents human achievement rather than failure.
- The flood is caused by divine anger.
- A god warns that the flood is coming and tells his hero how to build a boat. (This happens in the Hindu story too—Vishnu becomes a fish and tells Manu to build a boat.)
- The hero carries his family and animals on the boat.
- Three birds are released to check if the flood's subsiding. (Three, like the sides of a rigid triangle, often represents divine certainty.)
- After the flood, the boat is left on top of a mountain.

- Then a rainbow appears in the sky. But in Gilgamesh, the rainbow appears as the result of a goddess throwing her diamond necklace up in the air.

Which story sounds more *mythological* now, Gilgamesh or the Bible—necklaces or rainbows? And which contains those unexpected details that make it sound like truth?

Finally, we have the results of scientific exploration corroborating the story of Noah's flood:

- Early civilization is thought to have centered around the Black Sea plain—a warm place, cut off from the Mediterranean during a mini-ice-age. As the Mediterranean Sea froze over and shrank, a river flowed east across the plain which would later become the Black Sea. Farming could well have spread through many cultures from here. And the plain itself would have constituted the whole of the known earth.
- Global climate change (global warming in the Bible!) at the end of the mini-ice-age would have caused the Sea to rise. Eventually it flooded across the Straits of Bosporus, crashing through the rocky land barrier. An incredibly dramatic and destructive flood would have ensued, at the end of which, the new Black Sea would drain west into the Mediterranean, instead of flowing east into now-vanished plains of dust.
- Explorers have found evidence of farming (seeds preserved in the mud) below the Black Sea. Around 5,600BC these cultivated lands must have become completely flooded in the space of less than a year to leave seeds behind.
- Meanwhile, the Straits of Bosporus still retain an eastward flowing current on the sea-bed, from the Mediterranean Sea back into the bowl of the Black Sea, reflecting the flow of that river long ago.

If we cling religiously to the (translated) words of the Bible account, without thinking of the people who were first given those words, we end up maneuvering through curious contradictions (two animals or seven, rain causes flood, etc.) with complex interpretations and explanations as we follow the story of Noah.

If we choose to call the Bible account a *legend*, we have to question (as do our questioning children) *why do we still believe it?*

Certainly the story has wise lessons for us, but we can find those lessons just as easily elsewhere...

But if, instead, we think the Bible gives a true account, then we agree with science that there really was a flood, a natural event in the world we live in. Miraculously, one man survived, guided by the voice and infinite mercy of God. Noah's wife and children were saved as well, rescued by Noah's faithfulness... which compels me to pray with hope for all the non-believing people I know; because they too might be saved, even though I might never know them to have acknowledged or listened to God. I love the Bible!

Do Bible stories owe more to mythology than to fact? I think not. I think they tell the truth, through the eyes of real people, guided by a very real God. That said, I'm sure that many of our interpretations (including my own) are myths and legend. But above all I think, whatever our personal take on the answer to this question, we should all do all we can to make sure our children understand; Bible stories are not the same as fairytales. They're more boring perhaps, and definitely more real.

> *I learned a lot about Noah's Flood from Ryan and Pitman's account of their investigations in* Noah's Flood.

# Faith and Tradition: Abraham, Isaac and Jacob

Of course, all those Biblical stories could still be just the much-loved traditions, distorted histories from the past, that the wise modern child has grown out of. Good stuff, perhaps, for an age gone by, but a new age is dawning, they tell us; the old world is changing... and the college-bound student has to wonder what makes this tradition mean more than anyone else's.

Even within Christian traditions, we find plenty of reasons to argue with each other—plenty of reasons for our studious children to see faith as *debatable*, before they even begin to debate it in college. You (and the college-bound student) must have come across at least some of these common questions:

- Was Jesus born in a cave? Did that mean his extended family in Bethlehem defied (Jewish) tradition and refused to shelter his parents? Did three kings visit the cave, or did an untold number of wise men visit a house? And what is a "wise man" anyway?
- Was Peter the first pope? What did Jesus mean by saying he would build his church "upon this rock" (*Matthew 16:18-19*)? And is confession priestly or private? Why did Jesus say "whosoever sins ye retain, they are retained" (*John 20:23*)?

Exposed in college to different Christian traditions, the student might conclude (quite reasonably) that our disagreements are man-made; might deduce that our points of agreement are man-made too; and might *throw the baby out with the bathwater* perhaps.

So how do we protect those life-giving truths behind our traditions? Refusing to let our children ask questions doesn't help—they simply conclude that we're afraid of the answers... and that looking into the Bible won't give them any answers either. But the Bible is more than tradition, and our traditions are much, much *less* than what the Bible says.

Tradition isn't just a New Testament problem of course. Tradition colors how we read Old Testament stories too. It colors and differentiates those three faiths that, today, herald Abraham as our historical / spiritual *father*. Jewish, Muslim and Christian, we each claim as sacred the same physical part of the world, and we each put our own interpretations on the stories of that place. Sometimes we agree with one another. Sometimes we disagree. And sometimes—yay!—we even agree with history and science.

The background to Abraham's story is an interesting place to being looking at tradition. The names, customs and cultures depicted in the Bible are entirely in line with other contemporary documents and archeological discoveries. Sadly the way those scenes are depicted in traditional art or children's storybooks may not be quite so convincing though. Rembrand's painting of Abraham with the angels, showing Sarah looking out from the door of a house, doesn't quite fit how the Bible describes Abraham's tent. But that's tradition; the Bible, in contrast, describes real people living in a real historical world—with a real God guiding them.

In Abraham's case, the real man lived in a tribal world where inheritance was vitally important. Modern *tradition* dates Middle Eastern conflicts back to those ancient times, with Abraham's two sons, born of rival mothers, fathering descendants doomed to eternal war. But the Bible account of their tribes is a little more nuanced. Isaac and Ishmael can't have been estranged, even two generations later, since in *Genesis 28:9*, Isaac's grandson tries to appease his parents by marrying a woman of religiously acceptable lineage. He finds, courts and marries Ishmael's daughter (a daughter of his old age perhaps).

Then there's Abraham's other *son*, the orphaned nephew Lot who surely grows up like a son to his uncle. In *Genesis 11:27-31* we find Lot traveling with the clan from Ur to Haran (a place that's named, appropriately, after Lot's dead father). When Abram's father Terah decides to stay in Haran, Lot moves on with Uncle Abram and Aunt Sarai, living with them into adulthood. Eventually Lot settles in the fertile plains, close to the enticements of a nearby city, while Abram continues his nomadic life in the hills.

City life, of course, posed as many problems to faith then as now. City traditions were different from those Lot grew up with. City laws were made by kings; city taxes were raised by kings needing armies to defend themselves. Armies offered the lure of unrestrained power. And power corrupts—a truth as valid now as it ever was.

Lot's "cities of the plain" (*Genesis 13:12*) and their kings were subject to the great King Chedorlaomer. But, tempted by power and the desire to avoid paying taxes, they rebelled. As a result, their leaders and young men were taken prisoner in war and marched away, with Lot among them.

Perhaps the fleeing refugees told Abram of his nephew / son's fate. Then Abram gathered his nomadic friends and hurried to Lot's aid, rescuing the prisoners and, in passing, sharing a sacrifice of bread and wine with the priest-king Melchisedek.

Two points in this story have always intrigued me—and being intrigued might be one of the first steps to recognizing the difference between *baby* and *bathwater* when it comes to tradition.

- Melchisedek is described as "king of Salem," (*Genesis 14:18*) a place which seems likely to be the future Jerusalem. Standing on a hill, it would offer a good vantage point from where Melchisedek could watch the battle without joining in.

    But Melchisedek is also "the priest of the Most High God," though clearly not a member of Abram's tribe. So maybe belief in the God of the Bible was still a significant force in those ancient times, even if the stories were beginning to be corrupted into tales of multiple gods.

    Within a couple of generations, Abram's descendants would be isolated from the rest of the world, ready to solidify their beliefs without external influence. Meanwhile, I like to imagine true stories of the Most High God, stories that would eventually be written in the Bible, still circulating in the streets of cities like Salem… and Babylon.

- Secondly, the people running away from the battle were hindered by "slimepits" (*Genesis 14:10*), a curious detail I never even noticed on first reading. Slimepits, or tar pits in other translations, indicate the presence of volcanic activity. Within just a few years, this activity, or some other fiery fate, would overwhelm the cities of the plain in the famous destruction of Sodom and Gomorrah.

After the battle, Abram's wife grew tired of waiting for God's promised baby. She came up with a very Egyptian solution to her childlessness—an idea suggested perhaps by her Egyptian maid, Hagar, who she'd acquired during one of Abram's sojourns in Egypt.

Egypt, with its Nile-fed fertility, was indeed the place people usually went to for respite during famine, just as the Bible says. And surrogate pregnancy was not an uncommon practice there. But Hagar's pregnancy distressed poor Sarai, causing trouble, as human solutions born of human impatience so often do. Still, Hagar was comforted by God's promise that her son would be powerful and would grow up safe with his family.

*Genesis 16:16 and 21:5 are separated by quite a lot of chapters in the Bible, suggesting a rather long period between the births of Ishmael and Isaac. So Ishmael really did grow up safely with his family—he wasn't kicked out as a little boy, despite the images of tradition.*

Fourteen years later (a small enough number that people could count that far) Isaac was born. Far from the destructive and jealous little boy of tradition, Ishmael was almost an adult by then. When family arguments resulted in him and his mother being sent away, young Ishmael went off to marry an Egyptian, a woman from his mother's heritage, fathering a tribe of twelve sons. Most likely he moved south of the family home, just as Lot moved west on growing up. But there's no indication that Ishmael didn't maintain friendly relations with his father and brother (though not with his stepmother of course!).

Abraham (now renamed, as was not uncommon in those times) took another concubine after Sarai died. With Keturah, he fathered several more children. His heir, as promised, was Isaac, son of Sarah, but Ishmael and the other children received gifts of property (serious gifts, since Abraham was seriously rich). The two primary sons, Isaac and Ishmael, far from being sworn enemies, were the only ones to stand at their father's grave.

*Genesis 25:1-9 reveals an old man living out his life with another wife, and two favorite sons standing together at his death.*

Ishmael's children appear in the Bible story again, of course. Esau, realizing his foreign wives have displeased his parents, decides to marry Ishmael's daughter (*Genesis 28:9*). Clearly the tribes were still close enough for this to be a *good move*. Later still, Joseph, son of Jacob, son of Isaac, was sold to Ishmaelite traders (*Genesis*

*37:25*). The tribes were clearly still content to pass through each other's territory without fear. So much for that tribal warfare *traditionally* born of Abraham's two sons.

But what happened in those long chapters and years between Ishmael's and Isaac's births? Lot was enjoying the good life in Sodom, and Ishmael was growing up to be a fine young man, when three strangers came to visit the patriarch's tent. One of the strangers stayed to warn Abram that Sodom and Gomorrah were about to be destroyed. Meanwhile, the other strangers visited Lot.

Modern tradition uses this story to show how God hates sexual sin. But *Judges 19:14-30* puts the tale in a rather different light. The sins of Sodom and Gomorrah were not unique to those cities or to that time (or to today). The streets at night were (and often are) a dangerous place. So the strangers are urged not to risk staying out, but to rest at a citizen's house; this was the norm in any civilized place.

We all know what happens next to Sodom and Gomorrah—fire and brimstone, right? But remember the story in *Judges.* It's a dark tale, where a young woman is handed over to the rabble to be raped, just as Lot offers his daughters. In Judges the woman appears to be brutally murdered as well. But no fire and brimstone rained on Gibeah. *Does God not see? Does He not care?* (And do we not read, nor let our children read these stories as they grow up? But they're part of the Bible, and perhaps the truth isn't as simple as it seems.)

Sodom and Gomorrah and the cities of the plain lay in a volcanic place surrounded by bubbling bitumen pits. Perhaps their approaching disaster was a natural event in our natural (fallen?) world? Perhaps the miracle is, again, not that many people died, but that any survived. And perhaps our children should be allowed at least to ask about this, lest they conclude God stopped caring about rape and murder by the time of *Judges.*

In the end, Lot wasn't saved for his goodness—what *good* man would offer his daughters to a mob?—but by his uncle Abram's prayers.

I'm not an archeologist. I don't know how up to date my information is. But I've heard that archeologists might have found the Bible's "cities of the plain." Their excavations have uncovered buildings burned from the rooftop down, suggesting that fire fell from the sky. They've found a plain dotted with pillars of salty rock—what an amazing thought! Can't you imagine Lot rushing back to investigate when he realizes his wife has disappeared. He probably thought she was right behind him all the way. But now he returns to find pillars like people turned to salt as they fled the conflagration. Concluding his wife has been turned to salt too, he deduces it's her punishment for looking back.

Tradition led me to expect a single pillar, not a plain filled with pillars of salt. But our traditions were based on too little information. Not every detail was listed when the history was recorded. Some things were left for us to discover and marvel over later—real pillars of un-mythological salt!

Abram's visits to Egypt, his (and his son's) attempts to call a wife a sister, the digging of wells and making of treaties, Abraham's attempt to sacrifice his son (Isaac according to Jewish and Christian reading, but Ishmael in some Muslim writing), even the names of the Biblical characters, all fit with what has now been discovered of life in Bible times. History and the Bible really do agree, even when history and tradition begin to fall out. And our faith is not in tradition; our faith is *not* tradition. Our faith is in the very real God who reveals himself in these tales of our traditions.

One final trip to find food in Egypt, in the time of Abraham's great grandson, ends with the Israelites invited to live in Egypt's despised hill-country. There they kept their *dirty* flocks, while *real* Egyptians farmed the fertile plains. Isolated for 400 years (or thereabouts—who's counting), these people told God's stories around the fire and kept their faith pure and free from the world's contamination. No fanciful Egyptian mythologies for them.

Rabbinic tradition tells us the Israelites stayed in Egypt until around 1300 BC, after being enslaved by Pharaoh to build his new capital city, Rameses (*Exodus 1:11*). Christian traditions often choose an earlier date, around 1450 BC, because the Bible says there were 480 years between the establishment of Aaron's priesthood and the construction of Solomon's temple. Except the Septuagint says 440 years, and… well… maybe it's time to look at some math as well. Meanwhile…

If science and tradition disagree in their interpretation of a Bible story, which should we follow? Perhaps we'll each be called to a different view, a different *tradition* maybe, and perhaps we should each respect each other's views. Believing Moses lived in 1300BC won't stop anyone from also being sure God loves and saves us. If arguing that he must have lived in 1450BC risks making someone lose their faith, it's an argument any Christian should be more than happy to lose. And in heaven, thankfully, we'll know the truth.

*For more about archeological finds in the Bible lands, read Randall Price's* The Stones Cry Out.

*For more about differing traditional views of Abraham, read Bruce Feiler's* Abraham.

# Faith and Mathematics: Numbers

Would you ever imagine that math could be connected with faith? I don't mean the math of people who look for secret codes in the Hebrew letters of the Old Testament, adding, subtracting, multiplying... then claim they've defied statistics when they've more likely *deified* interpretation. I just mean real math, real numbers, and real analysis.

My brother gave a speech before the toast at our parents' Ruby Wedding (their fortieth wedding anniversary). It was a very good speech—my brother has an amazing talent for amassing, organizing and delivering vast quantities of fascinating facts and anecdotes. But every once in a while he needed a moment to gather his thoughts. These moments were easily recognized by the mantra, "Forty years is a very long time," which he repeated endlessly, to much amusement. (We reminded him of this mercilessly when he reached his fortieth birthday.)

Forty years really was a very long time in ancient cultures though. If you think about counting with the fingers on your hands, ten years is the most you can reach. Use your toes as well, perhaps, and you'll make it to twenty. Use your spouse's fingers and toes to get you to forty...

More realistically, one to ten might be considered countable numbers while anything higher is probably a guess. Ten, not surprisingly, is symbolically the number of a man (ten commandments for example, but look at all the other tens in the Bible—even in Revelation where trials and tribulations will last ten days (*Revelation 2:10),* or when ten thousand times ten thousand circle the throne *Revelation 5:11*). But the child, at ten, isn't quite a man, so some bigger, unspecified number might be needed for adulthood—for a generation perhaps. Meanwhile, four—four corners, four winds (four beasts in *Ezekiel 1:5* and *Revelation 4:6*)—is the number for the earth. So a young adult, a child grown up to an age of earthly usefulness, might be given the generational (numerical) age of four times ten.

We're told that Moses was 40 years old when he murdered a guard and ran away from Egypt. Fighting with the guard seems a pretty foolish, young-adult / pampered-teen kind of action, rather than that of a mature 40-year-old, but what if he wasn't yet mature? At age 80 Moses returns to set his people free. Skeptics might call his age impossible, while believers hail a miracle. The hopeful declare there's life after 79 after all. And the mathematician...? If 40 is the number assigned to a generation, perhaps Moses was really two generations old—only two times 25, not two times 40, after all. But will we allow our children to think of this, or will we insist that Moses looked like an 80-year-old great-grandfather?

Another forty comes soon afterward in the Bible. Remember the forty years of wandering in the desert, or was that a generation, or was it both?

*If you read Numbers 32:13 you might have to say both.*

If only one generation of people died as they wandered the desert, and if the early Israelites expected a similar lifespan to that of other tribes, we ought to guess they lost only 25 years before entering the Promised Land. In that case, Moses was only 25 when he fled; only 50 when he returned with his grown-up sons, and 75 when he died. Suddenly the impossible sounds more like real life and less like a miracle—more like a reason for unbelievers to accept the Bible's history, and less like a reason for believing children to turn around and call their faith a myth. That's got to be a good thing hasn't it? (Ah, but we do love our miracles…)

Meanwhile, back to the date of the Exodus. Will Jewish (1300BC) or Christian (1450BC) tradition win the day when we apply a touch of math?

While most Bibles say there were 480 years between the Exodus and the Temple, the Septuagint (Greek translation of the Bible) says 440 years. It looks (to a mathematician) as if someone multiplied a number of 40s (11 or 12) and got the answer wrong. (How very like me that would be—I love numbers and symbols, but I'm seriously poor at getting the right answers.)

If the Exodus really occurs while Rameses (*Exodus 1:11—Raamses and Pithon*) is being built, we might look to archeologists to resolve our problem—unless of course, we're unwilling to accept information that doesn't come from the Bible. Modern archeologists are pretty sure Rameses was built around 1300 BC (agreeing with Jewish tradition). But they date Solomon's Temple's to 960 BC, giving a time in between that's clearly less than 480 years. Which leaves readers to ask, which is right, science and history or the Bible?

Obligingly, the Bible actually helps us out in this one. We're given three lists of names for high priests holding office between these two events—*1 Kings 4:2 plus Ezra 7:1-5, 1 Chronicles 6:50-53,* and *1 Chronicles 6:3-13*. Surely we can use these lists to corroborate the timing—if only the lists were consistent with each other. But they aren't—so the doubting teenager asks, does the Bible contradict itself? I guess the Christian answer *should* be "No." But perhaps a wiser answer might be, "Let's look a little deeper."

Luckily, or by divine intent, these lists are perfectly consistent with the action of scribes copying ancient texts and including an occasional copying error—read them yourself and see. Combining the lists and removing what must surely be a repeated line, you'll be left with just 12 names—12 priests for 12 generations...

Are you thinking 12 times 40 now, where 40 is that generic *big number* representing a generation? If you are, then 480 years looks more like an approximation (12 times a generation) than a mathematical calculation (12 times 40).

Today, archeologists reckon ancient generations really were around 25 years. Using this estimate, instead of 40, the time from Exodus to Solomon's Temple, as counted by the list of 12 intervening priests, becomes 360 years. Is it surprising that this number so perfectly corroborates archeology and the Bible? Or is it math?

Meanwhile, my aunt celebrated her hundredth birthday, a seriously big number for sure. And the Bible's (big) hundreds and thousands offer another instance where math provides an answer to *myth*, in this case the *myth* of the enormous tribe.

Still looking at Moses, we're all familiar with the ten plagues of Egypt (can you recite them? In order?—science makes wonderful sense of them too, in the next chapter). Then Moses said "Let my people go," and led the Israelites to the Promised Land. But do you remember how many people there were?

The book of Numbers, appropriately named, makes an attempt to count the tribes, and the results are quite... scary... Various

Christian books describe how the Israelite crowd was so large it could be seen from space. The people marched in the shape of a cross, visible to watching angels, and foreshadowing Jesus—which is all very interesting and inspiring. But non-believers, and students just learning to question, will counter that the tribe simply couldn't have been so large.

*Read Numbers 1:45-46 and you end up with 603,550 men over the age of 20! Over half a million on one march?*

603,550 is a *very* precise number isn't it? And that's just the men of an age to fight in this tribe. It makes for an army bigger than the whole Egyptian army, bigger than several wandering Amalekite armies all put together. It makes for a total population of over 2 million people (adding in women and children), and they were served by only two midwives?

Looking back at those 400 years since they entered Egypt (when an earlier census was made), this is a nation where every woman has given birth to around a hundred live children before she dies. Do you feel scared yet? Or just dismayed? But wait.

*Now read Deuteronomy 7:7, Exodus 17:10-12, and ask yourself, were they really such a huge tribe?*

If they weren't a numerous people, if the Amalekites nearly overpowered them, how many were in this tribe?

The census in Numbers starts by listing the men in each tribe, and the thousands under them. But the word used for *thousand* is 'eleph, which can also translated as *troop*. (Alas for tradition, it sometimes *is* translated troop, but usually it isn't.)

We're told that the book of Numbers was written by Moses, but it's probably safe to assume other writers compiled it from pages and papyruses of Moses' writing. (Let's assume at the same time that Moses didn't write the account of his own death.) This later transcriber would have had the task of putting all the figures together. Perhaps the writer was also a mathematician—I'd love to find mathematicians in the Bible! And perhaps the writer, being better than I am at calculation, decided to add up all the numbers, rather than leaving readers to work them out. Taking 'eleph to mean thousand, and feeling very proud of the size of his tribe, the writer might conveniently forget God said they were small; he might not remember they were almost defeated by one small Amalekite army.

The numbers come out rather differently if 'eleph means troop and we assume a troop, like a slave work-troop, to be about ten people. Then we have 5,550 men age 20 and over, giving a tribe of about 20,000. Not surprisingly, this is pretty average in history and in the present day for a nomadic tribe. They could wander the desert without being totally weird, and God's word makes human sense.

So what will you do when a neighbor complains that there couldn't have been so many people in the tribe of Israel? Will you call it a miracle and send them away frustrated? Or will you let them do the math with you, then invite them to read the story for themselves? There's lots of great stuff in the Bible if we can just encourage people to read it instead of turning them away. And God will never let his Word return empty.

Like I said, I really do love numbers and math, but I really am hopeless at adding up. I've taken all those figures from Professor Charles Humphrey's excellent book, *The Miracles of Exodus*. Most of my information in the next chapter is from his book too. It's highly recommended and totally unpreachy. You might want to find a copy to loan to that hypothetical neighbor or your wandering teen.

Meanwhile, is it wrong to "reinterpret" the Bible's math?

*Read 1 Kings 7:23. The ratio of the circumference to the diameter of a circle is well known to be pi, not three, as indicated here.*

If Kings is right, then pi is three, and much of what drives modern life (including tires on cars) is incalculably wrong. If we're going to maintain that pi is approximately 3.142, we have to *interpret 1 Kings 7:23* in the light of math and the limits of ancient measurements and language. At which point, we might also allow interpretation of Numbers in a similar light. Meanwhile, however we choose to interpret those numbers, let's not push potential believers (or mathematicians) away from God's true faith.

> *If numbers are your thing, you might really enjoy the Mathematical Postscript in John Polkinghorne's* Belief in God in an Age of Science.

# Faith and Magic: Exodus

Modern Jewish traditions, and many Christian ones too, view the story of Exodus through a lens of religious fiction rather than math. They see it as good theology told in the form of a powerful legend, thus side-stepping the accusation of impossibility by agreeing it probably didn't happen. It's a tempting approach, for sure. But what if we look behind the scenes of the legend and learn that it looks like fact? What if those weird and wonderful miracles turn out to be science, not magic? And what if the story ends up seeming so historically, geographically, and geologically convincing it almost has to be true? Will that be evidence for God's hand in the world? Or will we complain that it's evil and wrong to explain our miracles away?

Teens grow up and lose their love of childish things. It's meant to happen that way. They stop believing in magic, and we beg them to see miracles. But how will they know the difference?

Lots of events seem magical in Exodus of course—bushes burn without burning up, sticks turn into snakes, a corridor of dry land crosses the raging Red Sea. But, as the science fiction writer, Arthur C. Clarke, once pointed out, "any sufficiently advanced technology is indistinguishable from magic." Perhaps any sufficiently inexplicable events will seem like magic too. It doesn't mean they *are* magic. And perhaps today we have better tools to understand and explain what's going on.

Maybe the events of Exodus looked like magic to their first readers and writers. Maybe that's why they sounded like magic when they wrote them down. But if we give our children that pat answer—God's miracles are good and Egyptian magic is bad—we set them up to reject both as they grow up. Is it really as simple as saying God works miracles, and man or the devil works the rest? What do you think?

While you're thinking, try remembering the miracles Jesus performed in the New Testament. It's interesting to ask which ones made the biggest impression on the people close to him. What made people think this was more than just watching another traveling magician? Imagine Jesus...

- ...healing the sick just like the Greek physicians do (magic, surely, in the eyes of the uneducated),
- ...turning water into wine like the Egyptian magicians do (they had their techniques and mysteries),
- ...directing fishing boats toward fish (a task any fisherman might undertake every day), and...

*Read Matthew 8:23-27. Why were the disciples so amazed at this after all the other things Jesus had done?*

The miracle that made the disciples truly marvel was the one that no magician, physician or fisherman could copy—God's control over nature. Historically, it was always so. God's control over nature impressed the Jews far more than more mundanely *magical* events in a world filled with Egyptian magicians practicing their arts. So maybe that's the difference between magic and miracles—it's a question of who's in control. And we never grow out of needing to know the answer.

Back in Egypt, Moses seemed eager to take control, but his efforts failed. Murdering the guards really wasn't God's plan. So as a mere 40-year-old (or perhaps at 25) he fled to faraway Midian where he got married, had kids, and 40 (or 25) years later met God.

We know where Midian was, but how did Moses get there, and why didn't the Egyptians stop him?

*The well in Exodus 2:15 would mark an oasis, village or farm.*

A trade route crossed the Sinai desert from Egypt to Midian, with the Red Sea's Gulf of Aqaba forming the boundary between nations. Moses would travel quickly on foot, possibly out-running any pursuit. Tradition has him travelling for ten days, corresponding to what would be a seven day journey across the desert and three days down the coast, stopping at wells on the way. Finally he rested by a well in Midian where he believed he'd reached safety. It's interesting that the Israelites also fled for seven days across the desert to the Red Sea, then three days down the coast to the wells at Marah (*Exodus 15:22-23*). Were they heading for the same place?

Moses marries a priest's daughter in Midian—presumably a Midianite priest—and looks after his father-in-law's flocks. Meanwhile, it appears, he fails to maintain his Jewish heritage. His sons aren't circumcised (*Exodus 4:24-26*) and he doesn't recognize God's voice when he hears it, asking instead, effectively, "Which god are you?"

Years pass and that fateful summer arrives. As usual in the desert's heat, Moses leads his father-in-law's sheep to good, presumably less over-heated pastures... but where are they?

*Read Exodus 3:1. Which mountain was this?*

*Modern* (4th century initially, becoming popular after the 15th century) tradition says Moses went back across the Gulf of Aqaba all the way to the *modern* Mount Sinai, in the Sinai desert. It's not a particularly good place to take sheep though—Moses' father-in-law might not have approved. But there are older traditions than these, traditions still followed by present-day tribespeople who live in the same area. These traditions and tribes suggest Moses marched eastward instead, to volcanic mountains where the weather is cooler and the pasture's good. So perhaps the *ancient* Mount Sinai of the Bible isn't on the *modern* peninsula after all. And perhaps we don't need to wonder why Moses marched in the wrong direction with those sheep.

Since the mountains were volcanic, they'd naturally be associated with *gods*, and the god of the Midianites was called Sin, hence Sinai. (Incidentally, this might also be why the Bible keeps changing the name to Mount Horeb, in order to avoid repeated references to a foreign god.)

Of course, on a volcanic mountain, a bush might appear to burn without burning up. If Moses' story were written in a non-Biblical context, educated readers might insist this recounts an occurrence on a volcano. Indeed, if it wasn't part of the Bible, the whole Exodus account would be hailed as one of the first written accounts of volcanic activity. Descriptions of God's appearance on Mount Sinai would be the most amazingly vivid first-person records of a volcano. But we'll come to that...

For now we come to magic. Moses asks God who He is. God replies and gives Moses a task. Moses tells God he can't do what God commands, and asks God for a sign. Then God gives Moses a staff with *magical* powers. But what was really so special about this staff (apart from the fact that he loaned it to Aaron later on)?

*Exodus 7:10-12 offers a nice fun magical story.*

Is it a miracle when the staff turns into a snake, or is it magic? Or neither perhaps? There really is a snake which looks stiff and straight like a rod if you hold it the right way. Not surprisingly, it turns back into a wriggly snake when you let it go. Egyptian magicians knew all about this as part of their training. They might have been disturbed when Moses' snake ate theirs—it might even have been a miracle of God's perfect timing, of God's control over nature. But Moses' staff wasn't miraculous or inexplicable from the magicians' point of view. So the Pharaoh didn't let the people go, and the plagues began.

Have you ever tried to remember the ten plagues in order? I used to find it as impossible as trying to remember the days of creation. Why do frogs come before flies? What's the sky turning black got to do with anything? And where do fish come into it? But after reading Professor Humphrey's book on Exodus, I can probably recite the plagues in the right order, after only a few moments thought, because now because they make sense—they make *scientific* sense. Is that heresy? If our children tell us it makes sense, will we reply that it's heresy, thus making them heretics?

1. **Red water and dead fish:** The magicians could do this (*Exodus 7:22*). The Nile became red every year in late summer from the sudden swift flow down the mountains. Ancient documents even describe it as "the river is blood," though predicting precisely when this would happen was hard. Fish weren't meant to die in the red water of course, but these days we've all heard of poisonous red tides. All this is taking place at Rameses (Qantir) on the Nile Delta, where a red tide *could* coincide with red floodwater, killing the fish. It *could* happen at exactly the right time for Moses, if it's a miracle; if God has control over nature.
2. **Frogs**: The frogs appear seven days after the red water (*Exodus 7:25*), which gives just the right length of time for fish to die in a red tide. The Nile would teem with frogs by late September and early October—the time of red tide—so vast numbers of frogs would now flee the polluted waters and cover the land.

3. **Insects**: The frogs couldn't get enough fresh water so they died and didn't eat the flies. *Exodus 8:16-18* tells us this was the first time the magicians couldn't copy the miracle.
4. **Flies**: The "lice" or gnats might be tiny flies feeding on decaying fish and frogs—what a delightful image. Then bigger insects come and start biting people.
5. **Dead animals**: Professor Humphreys looks at which animals died—only hoofed ones, no cats for example, even though we're sure the Egyptian royals would have kept them (*Exodus 9:3*). Humphreys follows this discovery by investigating what viruses are spread by which insects. He concludes the animals were killed by a virus carried by mosquitoes, while the boils in the sixth plague were caused by stable flies.
6. **Boils**: These affect people and animals (but not the Israelites, probably because they live in the hills, away from water). *Deuteronomy 28:27,35* leads to Humphreys' deduction that these are caused by stable flies biting the feet.
7. **Hail**: The worst hailstorm to date in Egyptian history takes place now—we know about this sort of weather in the US these days.

*Read Exodus 9:31-32 and notice the level of detail.*

The names of the crops destroyed tells us this happens in February or March. It also makes this sound like a contemporary account; otherwise how would the writer get the crops consistent (unless the writer were very good at researching history and geography)?

8. **Locusts**: It's the right time of year for locusts by now, and the wet muddy ground would be perfect for breeding. Meanwhile Goshen, being geographically different, continues to be spared. According to Genesis, Goshen is good land for animals as opposed to crops, so it's probably hill-country. Since the Pharaohs chose to raid the Israelites for slave labor, the Israelites must have lived close to Rameses, which makes Goshen the hill country just behind the Nile Delta. More importantly, since it's hilly and not filled with grain, it was probably spared by the locusts.
9. **Darkness**: The ground is covered in chewed up stubble and the weather is dry. Dust-storms begin (in March or April), and

they'll be worse than ever because of what the locusts left behind.

*Exodus 10:21 invites the question: how do you feel darkness unless it's caused by thick flying dust?*

10. **Death of the Firstborn**: Humphreys even comes up with a natural explanation for this, which truly amazed and enthralled me. The Egyptians are obviously panicking by now. They'll have dragged whatever they can save of their grain into silos before the locusts came. But the hailstorm will have left the seeds damp, and locust feces may have contaminated that final layer—the layer on top. The dust-storm seals the air-vents causing a perfect environment for dire misfortune. And now the Egyptians ask their gods for help... by preparing a feast... which will be cooked with that last-in-first-out layer of contaminated grain.

Gods in general have a liking for first-born sons, and for healthy specimens in worship. So the Egyptians feed the first-born of their flocks and their families, and those feces-contaminated top layers of salvaged grain poison them all.

There are, in fact, very fast-acting poisons that might grow under such conditions, leaving the rest of the grain safe underneath. Meanwhile, the Israelites eat their own food and prepare to leave. Those Egyptians who want to throw in their lot with Israel eat at their houses too and are spared. (*1 Chronicles 4:18* shows at least some Egyptians traveled with the Israelites.)

Do these *scientific explanations* mean the familiar events aren't miracles (or magic) after all, or do they mean that God is lord of nature? For myself, I just found it confusing when the plagues looked like magic. Now they look like miracles of God in total control, and I'm awed, just as the disciples were. I may be wrong—you may be sure I'm wrong—but my faith becomes stronger and I'm awed by our God who predicts and controls and arranges all these events to fit His plan.

But... what exactly was God's plan in this? Just to "let my people go"?

*Does Exodus 5:3 sound permanent to you, or does it sound like they were going to come back?*

There was I, thinking Moses said "Let my people go," and he clearly meant *forever*, didn't he? But that's not what it says. So now I revisit (with Professor Humphreys) that trade route across the desert, the one Moses followed when he first ran away. It's seven days from Egypt to Midian, and in seven days the fleeing Israelites will be beyond Pharaoh's control. So Moses asks for a seven-day leave of absence. Pharaoh imagines it—three days outward bound, one day to sacrifice, and three days more for the return. If the Pharaoh believes they're doing just what Moses said, he'll expect his Israelites back around seven days later... by which time they'll be gone. This could be why Pharaoh waited so long before sending troops after them, but d'you suppose God told Moses to lie, to give His people a better chance of escape? Is lying okay?

I don't know a definitive answer to that (though obeying God seems like a very good idea). But whatever Moses told Pharoah, the Israelites set out, led by a column of fire during the night and of smoke during the day. And I'm looking to Professor Humphreys to answer another curious question: What's with the fire and smoke?

I used to spend ages as a child, trying to imagine what the column must have looked and sounded, or even felt, like. Did no-one think to run ahead, maybe walk around it, try to see what was hidden on the other side? Or see the angels carrying it?

But if the burning bush was on a volcano, and this is where Moses was to lead God's people... What if that volcano has finally passed from mildly interesting to seriously active? The *column* would then be smoke and flame shooting upward from Mount Sinai, showing the way. And if Sinai is actually east of Midian instead of on the Peninsula, a line on the map quickly shows how that roaring eruption would have *guided* the Israelites!

Humphreys traces the route the Israelites took, using hints from the Bible text and contemporary geography, and even linguistics. They head along the same trade route Moses took across the desert, a straight line almost, pointing toward Mount Bedr, East of Midian—it's a route that would be marked, for them, by gray smoke rising from the mountain in daytime and glowing red smoke in the night. They pay for water at oases using treasures the Egyptians handed over to them (placatory sacrifices for the Israelite god perhaps). They spread their flocks to either side of the road, where spring growth provides nourishment. And in seven days they're approaching the Gulf of Aqaba—the eastern fork of the Red Sea.

You've probably heard the controversy over where that Red Sea crossing really took place—the Hebrew words, translated as Red Sea in Greek, really mean Reedy Water (or muddy puddle as some would say). Critics argue that a *puddle* ran dry, because seas surely can't. But Humphreys' explanation fits the timing, and the sea, and the whole of the rest of the story. First he points out that the Gulf of Aqaba is red with coral and gorgeously red in the sunset. It's not hard to guess why Greeks might have called it the Red Sea. Then he shows a photograph of fresh-water reads growing at the edge of the Gulf's salt-water sea. No wonder, then, that the Hebrews might have named it the Reed Water. And when Hebrews translated their own scriptures into Greek, would they care more about translating the name or about naming the real-world location recognizably? What do you think? Allemagne or Germany anyone?

The road splits as they approach the Gulf of Aqaba. The Israelites probably followed a narrow pass down toward the water. When they reached the shore they'd have to turn north to the crossing, at which point they'd be heading temporarily away from the volcano. The pillar, not surprisingly, *moves* behind them.

*Exodus 14:19 always had me wondering why that might be.*

But at this point too, Pharaoh has realized his slaves aren't coming back. The soldiers he's sent to chase them race down the pass, and things get scary. Meanwhile, Pharaoh's chariots rush along the other road. Turning south at the water's edge, they head back down the Gulf—a whole new meaning to *heading them off at the pass.* And now the Israelites stand surrounded, mountains to the west, sea to the east, chariots approaching from the north and soldiers from the south. So they pray. What happens next?

*Exodus 14:21 doesn't just say God made a path through the water; it tells us precisely how He made a path.*

The Bible says a strong east wind blew, which might mean anything blowing from the northeast, east or southeast. But the Gulf of Aqaba points northeast so we'll go with that. A strong wind blowing straight down the gulf, all night long, with just the right force, could cause what's called a *bore*. The water stands still, flowing down and being blown back with equal effect, so dry land is revealed. Of course, such a wind would probably be accompanied by quite severe weather—and three days later the weary Israelites will come to wells where they've been promised fresh water, only to find the sour taste of storm runoff. But for now, they march safely across the Red Sea, rejoicing in God's favor.

Remember the tradition that Moses, 40 years earlier, marched three days down the coast to where he finally stayed. No wonder the Israelites expected fresh water three days later. But no worries. Charcoal provides the perfect filter, and there are lightning-downed trees just waiting to be used.

*Read Exodus 15:22-25. Is this where Moses left his wife and sons with her father for a while (Exodus 18:1-5)?*

Humphreys continues to trace the Israelites' path using geographic clues. He combines the accounts from Exodus and Numbers with the names of places in non-Biblical documents, with archeological excavations, and with travel diaries. The result is a journey that follows a trade route south down the east coast of the Red Sea, then turns inland on a less-used route, leading eastward and upward to a desert, the Wilderness of Sin. Here, honey-like manna drips from bushes overnight, amazing amounts of water collect in the morning dew, and quail on their natural migration path fly in flocks big enough to sink ships.

*Exodus 16:13-15 shows God providing all the Israelites needed, but was it a miracle of provision or a miracle of perfect timing—perfect control over nature?*

Eventually the route leads to the volcanic mountains, where Moses strikes *the rock*.

*Read Exodus 17:6. I'd never quite realized the rock was* at *the mountain rather than simply on the way. But this makes sense if it's a volcanic mountain standing on a rock table (as Mount Bedr does).*

You really can get water from this type of rock. People still do today. A miracle of nature!

The Israelites settle in a comfortable pasture, where flocks are fed and watered, leaving enough water remaining for ritual cleansing.

There was a river on the rock plain under Mount Bedr—a likely site for Mount Sinai it seems. Then God appears.

*Read Exodus 19:18-19. What might this look like?*

Okay, I'm talking volcanoes. Maybe you're even imagining volcanoes now. Smoke, trembling ground, even trumpet-like sounds are all characteristic of volcanic eruptions. There's no lava, but that's not uncommon. It will still be dangerous to wander around, and the Israelites are warned not to go up the mountain. As Humphreys says, if this wasn't the Bible, archeologists would treasure it as the world's first eye-witness account of an eruption, which is pretty amazing, though clearly it's not the whole story.

And at this point, I should wrap this up. I guess I forgot to mention the Amalekites, who came to fight the Israelites at the mountain; perhaps they thought it was the mountain of their own god and didn't want foreigners taking over. (Remember, Sin?) Then there's Jethro, Moses' father-in-law, who knows exactly where to find Moses, since this is where he used to pasture his flocks. Jethro brings Moses' wife and sons with him too—they probably took the shepherds' route while the tribe needed something more like a road to follow with such a large crowd.

What else have I forgotten? The golden calf? The plague that was maybe attenuated in those who drank water with ground up gold in it? The earth opening up and swallowing all the rebels, as indeed might happen on volcanic ground?

Actually, the biggest thing I've forgotten is the ending of Humphreys' book. I read most of the way through without knowing if the author was a Christian—just following his scientific analysis and investigation made me thoroughly enjoy the journey. But in final pages the author asks his readers to choose what they believe. He's used modern science to explain every miracle in the Exodus story—clearly not magic! And he's shown how even the tiny details in the Bible corroborate its historicity, making it sound like an eye-witness account. The sequences of events all make sense. The consequences seem real. But for all of these things to take place, each at precisely the right moment, each unpredictable yet happening just as required—could that all be coincidence, every step of the way? Or is it actually both *easier* and *more logical* to believe there's a God controlling nature, a God who guides the destinies of mankind?

When I hear about magic, I want to know how it was done. But then it wouldn't be magic anymore. Miracles, however, really are different. Knowing how miracles might have been *done* leaves me in awe of God. Nobody else could do these things, no matter how hard they tried. And so I feel just like those disciples of Jesus—"even the wind and the sea," and insects, fish and frogs, and volcanoes obey Him.

Will we allow our children to share this awe? Or will we tell them it's wrong to *explain away* miracles, leaving them to choose between a God of magic or no God at all? Whatever we believe lies behind the Exodus story (and we can none of us be sure), let's not allow a humanly religious certainty to blur the difference between magic and miracles. Our kids don't need to agree with our idea of the miraculous—but we want them to have faith in a God of miracles.

> *For more about the miracles of Exodus, I strongly recommend Colin Humphrey's wonderful book,* The Miracles of Exodus.

# Faith and Law: Leviticus

Most Christians remember the picture of Moses coming down the mountain, two tablets of stone in hand with the Ten Commandments written on them. According to tradition, when Moses sees the people worshipping a golden calf, he throws the tablets of the Ten Commandments down and promptly breaks them. But according to the Bible, the Ten Commandments were already written in the Book of the Covenant...

*Exodus 24:4-7 shows Moses presenting the Commandments to the people, and dedicating them to obedience.*

The story about Moses throwing tablets on the ground comes more than forty days later.

It's a great image though, broken tablets for broken laws and a broken relationship with God. Our Creator cares enough for created people that He meets us and writes the rules of how we're meant to be. God cares enough about those rules that He threatens destruction of His people. God cares enough about law, and we should care too.

The bit we sometimes forget is that God cares enough to send His son because *no* laws, not even God's own handwritten laws chiseled onto mountain stone, can save us. Because only love will save. Then we campaign for our governments to make *more* laws. Who do we think we are saving? And who will we lose?

According to the Bible, God speaks to Moses several times while he marches the Israelites toward Mount Sinai. When they finally arrive, God speaks from a cloud, giving the people three days to prepare and cleanse themselves for His appearance. Luckily, we think there was a river near the mountain, assuming Colin Humphrey's conclusions are correct. Otherwise we'd need more magic and miracles to provide the water.

Afterward, God comes down onto the mountain in their sight, but the people mustn't try to touch Him or even touch the mountain (an injunction that Arab tribespeople still apply to Mount Bedr). On the third day the mountain trembles, clouds and lightning cover its summit, thunder and trumpets sound, fire and smoke pour out and the earth trembles. Moses goes up the mountain to speak with God and is sent back to bring Aaron with him. But no stone tablets have been mentioned yet. Moses and Aaron climb up together and receive the Ten Commandments, followed by instructions about building altars, freeing slaves, restricting the punishment for crimes... but no tablets... not yet...

*Exodus 21:24 isn't a Commandment, but it might be an explanation of how a commandment applies in everyday life.*

All these rules and instructions might be considered practical applications of the Ten Commandments. Then Moses and Aaron return down the mountain, and Moses (not God) writes God's words in the Book of the Covenant (*Exodus 24:4,7*), after which he leads seventy elders into the presence of God before climbing the mountain again, on his own (or possibly with Joshua).

And now, at last, Moses receives those famous stone tablets. Ironically, while he's so busy on the mountain, learning all about God's plan for Temple sacrifice (not for law at all), Aaron and the people lose hope that he'll ever return. It's been forty days (*Exodus 24:18*, that curious number 40 again)—too long to wait when it's clear Moses must have been devoured by the fire-god after all. They make sacrifices to a golden calf, which may be a well-wrought statue, or could equally just be a molten lump of gold that looks like a calf. In their defense, the calf is a symbol of the Midianite god Sin. *Sin* owns the mountain, according to tradition. So, if they threw their treasures into the flames and a calf-shaped nugget were pulled out, it might be *natural* to guess the god has come to claim his due. Then Moses hears the clamor of their singing and hurries back.

So Moses throws down the tablets, breaks them, and returns to ask for more.

Meanwhile, since this is a chapter on law, here are the Ten Commandments, as listed in *Deuteronomy 5*:

1. There is only one God and we must worship only Him.
2. We must not take the name of God in vain.
3. We must keep the seventh day holy as a Sabbath to God.

*These three are* God *commandments, where three is symbolic of God and certainty.*

4. Honor father and mother.

5. Respect life.
6. Respect marriage.
7. Respect property.
8. Respect the good name of your neighbors.
9. Do not be jealous of your neighbor's wife, and
10. Do not be jealous of your neighbor's property:

*Seven* people *commandments, where seven is symbolic of God's plan for creation.*

Are you confused? Is this really the same list of Ten Commandments that you learned as a child? The three and seven seem so beautifully symbolic to me. Having grown up Catholic, with the commandments numbered this way, I was startled to learn that Protestants number them differently. Combining my 9 and 10 into one (don't be jealous of any of your neighbors' property, including his wife), they split number 1 into two separate commandments: "1. Worship only one God," and "2. Don't make any idols."

So, looking at my ninth and tenth commandments, was my Catholic background feminist, refusing to consider that wives are just property? Or should there have been eleven commandments (maybe even twelve) instead? Did we all mis-number them, or miscount?

Alas, but ten is another Biblically symbolic number—the number of *man*, of the fingers on two hands, and of things that are limited and countable. All traditions seem to agree there are Ten Commandments, even if we don't number them the same.

*Exodus 34:28 actually says there were ten!*

Not that there are only ten laws of course: Jewish tradition counts 623 laws given to Moses, including those Commandments. Christians remember just ten (then add a few). And Jesus lists two.

*Read Mark 12:30-31. Love God, and love your neighbor.*

It's not hard to see how ten can be condensed into two. Equally, it shouldn't be hard to see how they were expanded to 623. There are dietary laws which helped people show love to their neighbors by keeping the community healthy (no pork, no goat-kids cooked in their mothers' possibly contaminated milk…). There are social laws which limit punishments for infractions (no compensation beyond the physical cost). There are ritual laws which bind the community together in worship of God. Above all, there are laws applicable to the social situation of the time, laws that provided for a nation which, in testimony to the efficacy of those laws, still lives today.

The one law of Genesis—don't eat the fruit of the tree of knowledge of good and evil—might not be so different from Jesus' laws either; demanding the right to determine right and wrong for ourselves is all too often how we fail to love God and our neighbor. Meanwhile, the Ten Commandments of Exodus form the foundation for much of Western legalism. But what of the other 613? Do we remember them? Do we want to remember them?

Jesus placed the meaning of the law higher than the letter, reminding listeners that "the Sabbath was made for man" (*Mark 2:27*). He deepened and sharpened the Commandments, declaring that furious anger was as criminal as murder, and lust as adultery (*Matthew 5:21-30*). But then he comforted the sinner with love, bearing our sins on the cross, reminding the disciples that neither the blind man nor his parents deserved the curse of blindness (*John 9:1-3*), and letting the adulterous woman walk free (not to mention alive *John 8:1-11*). Walking under a tree where a tax-collector hid, Jesus made himself a friend (*Matthew 9:9-13*) instead of demanding recompense and repentance.

The truth is, despite the Old Testament laws, so carefully and beautifully tailored by God Himself to fit His people's needs, the Jews still strayed—a lesson we tend to forget when we want our country to set laws agreeing with our moral interpretations. Law doesn't save.

The Bible is full of tales of God's own people breaking His law, and only love could save them—that same love which defined the laws of Temple sacrifice to fulfil humanity's need for verifiable forgiveness. In the New Testament, we see God's love personified in Jesus' sacrifice. And still we try to enforce *Christian* behavior by passing *Christian* laws. We expand the Ten Commandments to fit our own chosen rules and regulations. We campaign to have our rules endorsed and enforced by government, thus claiming for ourselves God's power to save society. We point our fingers at those who disobey *God's law* as interpreted by us. But God points to His son.

The truth is we are just as incapable as Adam and Eve, and just as incapable as Old Testament Jews, when it comes to obeying God's law. We are all sinners, saved not by obedience but by the love of God. When we value rules and regulations more highly than showing love to our neighbor, when we imagine our human rules and regulations might save where even God's law fails, when we campaign triumphally *against* abortion and *for* the death penalty, perhaps we should remember Eden's trees. And perhaps we should remember that our children might not agree with us; let's make sure we don't turn them away from God when we declare that God's on our side.

Paul's letter to the Romans begins with a description of a world not so unlike ours—one where whole communities know nothing of God. Whole societies imagine they live without Him. Whole religions are based on knowledge of self, not of Him. It's a broken world, a world of tsunamis, tornadoes and earthquakes, a world of global warming and loss of habitat, a world of sickness and plague, and a world where the natural order of humanity is changed, where children are born crippled or blind, where man no longer cleaves to his wife, where sexuality is warped, and nakedness leads to shame. Paul asks how that can be, when God is in control, and concludes…

*Romans 1:21-26. These things happen to our world because, though we "knew God [we] glorified him not as God... but became vain..."*

Perhaps if our world seems more fallen than the world of yesteryear, we should not condemn our neighbor so much as ourselves. Perhaps we should ask if we too have professed ourselves wise, imagining our laws all-wonderful, and failing to give God the glory which is surely His due. And perhaps we should be careful to remember and remind our children, we are saved by love, not law, and no human law can ever take God's place.

God's law of love never changes. God's Ten Commandments don't change. But God Himself began changing His 613 laws soon after the death and resurrection of Christ.

*Acts 10:9-16 shows God Himself changing the dietary laws.*

Did God alter the law so more people could come to faith? Or had man's understanding of food and diet improved enough to remove the need for the law? Strict dietary codes helped keep the early Israelites healthy. But now we have refrigerators; pork and shellfish are safe as long as we treat them with care; meat can be cooked with milk and there's no danger we'll cook the kid in its own mother's own milk (*Exodus 23:19*)... What else might have changed?

If some of our favorite *cultural Christian* laws aren't listed in the Ten Commandments, who decides what must still be obeyed? Should moldy fabrics be taken to the priest before they can be used again (*Leviticus 13*)? Should lambs be slaughtered when skin diseases are healed (*Leviticus 14*)? Should we wash all our clothes after touching a woman's chair at the wrong time of the month (*Leviticus 15*)? What about eating meat with the blood in it? (*Leviticus 17* and *Acts 15:29*)? And what about sexuality (*Leviticus 18*)?

What about our kids if they're not sure they agree with us? Can they still agree with God? Where does man's law end and God's law begin?

*Read Mark 12:29-31. And what can anyone add to that?*

> *To learn more about how the Old Testament laws applied so perfectly to Old Testament life, read the articles on Food, Health Care, Sickness etc. in Nelson's A-Z resource,* What does the Bible say About...

# Faith and War: Joshua and Judges

Many non-believing friends have condemned my Christian faith as something legalistic, divisive and dangerous, leading to wars. So many have been killed in the name of belief, they say, this must surely prove *faith* is anathema compared to love. They point to the Old Testament and claim we follow a vengeful God of war, unforgiving and cruel. How could a loving God demand that whole nations, whole civilizations, women and children and animals be wiped out? How could a loving God throw people from their homes and destroy their livelihoods? And how can I deny this is what God does? How can I deny it's what God does and what He allows—look at the *Troubles* in Northern Ireland; look at World War II? My God is not a good God they tell me—they who don't know Him. He's not a God they would choose to follow.

Meanwhile, there are well-meaning Christians who declare they'll believe the New Testament's loving God and ignore the Old, as if the one had any meaning without the other. (How could a good God sacrifice his Son?)

Did God change over time, as some people say today? Did God learn from His mistakes? (Does God *make* mistakes?) Did our perception of God change, which is what I used to say? Or are we just being selective in our reading and our understanding?

Perhaps it might be worth going back to read those unpleasant, war-torn chapters of the Bible to find out more. Because, after all, they *are* written in God's word; they're there the Bible...

The early Jews did indeed kill lots of people, including women and children; they destroyed whole tribes, laid waste to cities and tore them down to the ground... But this is only a part of the Old Testament story. The march from Sinai and the invasion of Canaan is a rather selective piece of an extensive whole, and if reading it troubles us, perhaps we, together with our children, might see our trouble as an incentive to read on, rather than an excuse to stop. If we believe, as we say, that God is good, it should be a powerful incentive.

The God who led the Israelites out of Egypt wasn't a vengeful God. He could have totally wiped out their Egyptian masters—He clearly had the power—but instead He let them continue in their own land while He led his people elsewhere.

The God who gave His people the Ten Commandments, before their march to Canaan, doesn't sound like a vengeful God either. He surely seems more like a wise and loving leader, giving rules to improve society—rules that have proven so powerful we still follow them today. He gave rules for health that protected His people through centuries of sickness and disease. He gave rules for worship that allowed them release from the pain of humanity's guilt.

But yes, God did then send His people back to the land He had promised them before. And this did involve conquest. And conquest involved war.

Just for reference, let's set the scene with a story of modern warfare. Suppose a couple of generations from now, someone reads a tale which describes the *conquest of Iraq*. In this story, American troops, guided by God, drive into Iraq. They surround the city where Saddam Hussein is hiding. They block the roads and announce that anyone who chooses to become American will be spared. Crowds and crowds leave the city, all chanting "We are Americans," and go free. Finally, when the city's almost empty, the soldiers march in and find Saddam Hussein cowering in a bunker. They say to him, "America forgives you," and let him go.

Would anyone believe that story? Why not?

If the Bible stories of Israelite tribes entering Canaan were similarly bloodless and forgiving, would you believe them? Perhaps the violence is a mark of authentic history rather than proof of a violent God. It's the violence inherent in this world and its people.

Modern understanding of tribal culture, historical context, geography, and yes, even military strategy, makes perfect sense of the Bible's account of the conquest of Canaan—it sounds authentic; it even sounds as if it comes from eye-witness accounts, and it's even preserved like eye-witness accounts:

*Read Joshua 8:32. If Moses wrote his original documents on papyrus, as he learned in Egypt, they could have been falling apart by now, hence the need for Joshua's rewrite—a nice authentic touch in the historical record.*

But what else happened between Moses receiving the law and Joshua recording it?

The Israelites appear to march straight from Sinai to Canaan after leaving the mountain. This would lead them to the Beersheba Valley where cities were fortified with strong walls, and standing armies of well-trained soldiers rode war-chariots across the plains. Chaim Herzon and Mordechai Gichon, in their book, *Battles of the Bible*, point out Moses' wisdom in sending respected leaders across the river to spy out the land. But these leaders return with evidence of things they've seen to support their reports (fruits etc.) and a declaration that the invasion is doomed to fail. In human terms it probably was, as the army that disobeys God's order soon learns (*Numbers 14:39-45*).

In the Bible story, God banishes the Israelites to the desert for 40 years (or a generation, which might be more like 25 years). In military terms, the Israelite army and people set off in search of a better route. The tribes to the east of Canaan have old associations with Abraham and Isaac—the Edomites, Moabites and Ammonites. Negotiating, and if necessary fighting, with them will be much easier. So the Israelites *wander* and slowly work their way to a point on the Jordan River much further north, near Jericho.

*Numbers 21:21-26 describes one battle along the way*

The Israelites obviously know where they're going as they *wander*—not so purposeless a journey as I'd imagined after all. Israeli Intelligence (remember those spies) may well have learned that Sihon has recently conquered the Moabite lowlands. Sihon won't have had time to regroup, so it makes sense continue north along the eastern edge of Canaan. And so they reach (and rest in) the sparsely settled land of Gilead. And the invasion starts again.

What does an army need first for a successful invasion? A bridgehead I guess, and crossing the Jordan from Gilead gave the Israelite tribes an excellent bridgehead—safe land behind them, good routes into easily defensible mountains, lots of fords where small armies can attack and retreat, and fertile land on which to settle and produce resources. But how would they cross—there's a fast flowing river ahead?

*Does Joshua 3:14-17 remind you of anything?*

The Bible tells us the River Jordan ran dry, just like the Red Sea. It even tells us how—starting with a mud-slide at Adamah, probably triggered by an earthquake; mudslides really do happen there, and really do make the river run dry. God works, again, through nature, and doesn't mind telling us so.

But crossing is only the start of the story. The great walled city of Jericho rules the plain, and Joshua, sensibly, sends spies to find out how big a problem this will be.

*In Joshua 2:1, Rahab might have been a harlot, but the same word means hostess and an inn would be a perfect place to gather intelligence.*

The spies learn that morale is low. They may also have found the walls of Jericho in poor repair, but that's not recorded in the Bible—it's inferred from history. The spies' report and God's guidance lead Joshua to send his people marching around the city walls. Eventually, famously, the walls fall down, whether from disrepair, another earthquake, resonance with the Israelite shout, or even because the enemy was lulled into hiding away while the Israelites broke them (yes, I'm looking for God working in nature again, but that's just me)... *Battles of the Bible* prefers the last approach, citing a successful strategy of lulling the enemy by getting them used to your maneuvers before you attack. But there are lots of possibilities. The point is, yes, this is war; yes, it is real; and yes, God cares about it.

The Judean mountains present the next obstacle for God's people. If Israel can conquer the mountains, their bridgehead by the river will be secure. Not only that, but the Egyptians (still using those major trade routes near the coast) and the Phoenicians (Egypt's allies on the coast) will be unlikely to waste time attacking Israel on the high ground.

In military terms, more battles are essential to make that stronghold. In spiritual terms, if God's people are to stay isolated from corruption, as they did before slavery in Egypt, invasion and securing the borders are essential too, which means more battles.

Bethel is the biggest town nearby and defends the watershed in the mountains. It ought to be Israel's next major target, but it's very well-defended. So the Israelites head first to the mountain town of Ai and the watershed's source. However, their initial, over-optimistic, frontal attack fails.

*Joshua 7:4 puts it very simply.*

Failure's not the same as defeat of course. The Israelite's second attack is more sophisticated and uses a two-pronged approach—one army hiding in the hills above Ai while the other pretends to attack and retreat, drawing out the defenders.

*Joshua 8:14-19 reads like a scene in a war movie.*

Once the enemy has been drawn far enough away, Joshua gives the signal. His hidden army, uphill of Ai, sets fire to the fort. The two branches of the Israelite forces then trap Ai's defenders between them, and the written report declares not a single enemy survived, as is the wont of written military reports, both then and in more modern times.

Of course, if no-one at all was left in the city (as seems to be implied, on modern reading), then the women and children in *Joshua 8:25* must have been part of the army, which seems unlikely. Clearly a large number of men and women were killed, in the army and/or the city. But reading in the light of history, many women and children would have fled to the hills as the city was attacked. Survivors would then try to join the Israelite tribes. This same approach—*you killed our menfolk and now you should care for us*—is still maintained in tribal warfare in the Middle East today, and has a lot to do with Western cultural misunderstandings there.

Joshua hangs the leader in full view of everyone, an action that makes perfect cultural sense at the time. Then in *Joshua 8:35,* he reads and writes the law to the "strangers that were conversant among them," to those new members of the tribe, just as might be expected.

It's war, it's violent, but it's possibly less violent then modern warfare where West meets East. Survivors, contrary to our Western cultural reading, are cared for and absorbed into the tribe. And the conquest continues.

Other tribes in the area naturally become concerned after the fall of Ai and Jericho. The Gibeonites trick the Israelites into an alliance, and end up providing slaves or aliens to work at menial tasks.

*Joshua 9:3-6 describes their sneaky approach.*

Other tribes, rather than attacking Israel, now attack Gibeon, thus testing not only the strength but also the trustworthiness of their enemy. Will Israel rush to its allies' defense?

Joshua's army sets out under cover of night and hides in the hills and forests round Gibeon—it's interesting that we think in terms of nations fighting nations, whereas this story is more a record of one tribal city against another—more like pre-European America than Middle-ages Europe.

The Ammonites would probably have camped near water, and the Israelite attack, at night, rushing down from the hillsides, was a big success. But it wouldn't help the invasion much, unless the fleeing forces could be killed before they regrouped—preferably before dawn. At which point we read that the sun stands still.

*Read Joshua 10:12-14. We remember the sun "hasted not to go down," but tend to forget, the moon did likewise.*

I'd always interpreted this story as God granting Joshua an incredibly long day in which to fight his foes, but the authors of *Battles of the Bible* point out that this would be singularly illogical in military terms. It's far more likely God granted them an over-long night by making the morning mists obscure the sun. After all, Joshua's army was good at, and armed for, hand-to-hand fighting in trees, while the enemy were armed for and accustomed to full-scale battle formations. History and geography reveal that thick mists do arise in the Ajalon valley, but, like the Jordan running dry, they can't usually be counted on to rise just when we need them.

Israel's enemies now try working together, determined to get through the mountains and reconquer the Jericho plain.

*Read Joshua 11:5-9. Poor horses!*

They combine and bring their armies, plus horses and chariots, to a staging point in the mountains ready to march on Israel's camp. But chariots are hard to use in mountain warfare. Joshua traps them before they can move onto the Israelite plain. Destroying the chariots and horses after the battle might seem strange, but the Israelites wouldn't have known how to use them—it's just the same as destroying cities that they don't know how to defend. Israel's enemies are far more advanced in terms of weaponry and siege craft. But Israel has numbers, wise strategy, and God on its side.

Of course, killing horses, burning cities, murdering women and children… this begs the question, did the Israelites really destroy everything and everyone in their path?

*Read Joshua 8:35, 9:23, 13:13, and Judges 1:19 and meet a host of* alien *Israelites.*

The Bible mentions "strangers" in the midst of the Israelites. Who could these be if not non-Israelites living among God's people? Who were the "bondmen" (*slaves* in other translations)? Ignoring arguments about slavery (a very different institution back then), it's clear there were plenty of survivors living among God's people. Reports of total destruction, like WWII counts of aircraft downed in war, may have been slightly exaggerated—or recorded as they first appeared in the heat of war, without later modification.

Meanwhile, there are cities "of the plain" not yet conquered because their towns have walls and their armies have chariots. The *country*, inasmuch as it was a country rather than land occupied by competing tribes with shifting alliances, has not changed hands. By the end of the book of Joshua, it's still a land occupied by competing tribes, some of whom happen to be Israelites.

Any history of that place and time is bound to be a story of war, and the history in Joshua is no exception. It's a book in the Bible, because we cannot read the spiritual history of a people without its human history too. And it rings so authentically true, from an historical point of view, that it makes those spiritual truths in the Bible shine as authentic too. I believe they are true. And I believe the God of the Bible was the same yesterday, today and forever. He guided the wars of His people then, as we pray He will guide ours now. And He longed for peace, as do we.

Battles continue, of course, far into the book of Judges. The Israelite tribes move down from forested highlands into the plains. The plainspeople fight back. The story of Deborah includes a very well-planned three-phase battle involving armies from several Israelite tribes (and a female leader—so much for the Bible being anti-feminist!). The story of Gideon takes place in a time of drought when enemy tribes take over the fields that feed southern Israel. The Philistines raid from the coastal plain, pushing into Canaan from the west as Israel has pushed from the east. Again, the enemy is more advanced than the Israelites—the Philistines know how to work with iron (*Judges 4:3, 1 Samuel 13:20*)—and again we're reminded these events take place in a real historical world, with a real historical Iron Age—even one where neighbors might sharpen your plowshare but not your sword. It's a real, historical, *changing* world. The time of tribes is ending and the age of nations begins... just about when the Biblical narrative tells us Israel has demanded a king—they demand to be a nation at last, not just an alliance of tribes.

It all makes sense, in military, historical and geographic terms—not a story of a vengeful God after all, but the story of real people, loved and guided by God in a very real world—a story that's equally relevant today, and a story that advocates obedience to a loving God over vengeful destruction. Let's *not* ignore the Old Testament wars. Let's *not* try to explain them away, to ourselves or to our children. And let's not emulate their evil either. Instead let's read and hear that startling ring of truth. God cares. God cared about a fledgling, foolish nation. And He cares about fledgling, foolish us.

Is the Bible, or the Old Testament, just a book about old wars, filled with violence and blood? Or is it a book about real people, really redeemed by God?

> *I learned more than I'd ever imagined about military strategies in the Bible when I read Chaim Herzog and Mordechai Gichon's excellent book,* Battles of the Bible.

# Faith and History: the Rise of Kings

Myth, analogy and fiction all have their place. They inspire, guide, confuse, bemuse us maybe, and they make for great reading. There's lots of great reading out there; but that's not what the Bible's about. If we try to convince people it's worth reading the Bible because it's a good book, we shouldn't be surprised that they prefer something else. But if the Bible is history, verifiable and true, then it's worth reading for the facts. And the facts might change the world. After all, anyone who reads the Bible's facts runs the *risk* of being inspired by the author too—a risk we Christians should be more than happy to hold out to family and friends.

World history passed through ages—Stone Age, Bronze Age, Iron Age and more. And the books of Samuel and Kings in the Bible reveal a new age dawning, the Iron Age when nations rise to take the place of tribes, armies carry iron blades, and Israel demands a king. Without historical context, "We want a king" seems a pretty random demand—nothing more, perhaps, than an artifice to teach our children about King Jesus. But in context, it's no artifice at all. Our children may be sure the world needs no kings today, but knowing that God was as active in the pre-king world as in the world of kingdoms just might inspire them to recognize His actions today in our post-kingdom reality.

The Philistines, living near the coast to the west of Israel, were originally seafarers. While the rest of the Middle East lingered in Bronze Age simplicity, they had already advanced in technology to the Iron Age. Israelite tribes accepted them as useful neighbors and more... Samson, a Danite, fell in love with Timnah, a Philistine, then fell out with her, precipitating war. It's the petty, normal stuff of life when tribes with different traditions share a land.

But God told the Israelites *not* to share the land. This didn't preclude other tribes being assimilated, as long as their people were willing to become God's people. But God did demand that the Israelites not make ungodly alliances—after all, to ally with a tribe was to ally with all its allies (and with their gods). God does not ally himself with those who don't believe in Him, nor with "gods" who are not God (*Exodus 20:1-3*).

The Jewish tribes didn't live up to God's laws of course. They warred with foreign tribes and with each other. They worshipped God on the same mountaintops that were claimed for foreign gods, frequently mixing their worship with other people's worship. And they generally failed to live as God intended, as do we all.

*Read Judges 17:6, 18:1, 19:1, and 21:25 (Read the rest of chapter 19 for a truly unpleasant story).*

Which kind of suggests, things would surely be better if they only had a king. So...

*1 Samuel 8:4-11 (and on) gives a vivid depiction of what kings will do.*

Does God want Israel to have a king or not? Does God change His mind? Can He be trusted? And does the Bible contradict itself when God tells them He's chosen their king?

Samuel is the last of Israel's judges. He fights the Philistines in the west, continuing the conflict of Samson's day, while Ammonites attack from the east, across the Jordan. In human terms, this loose confederation of Israelite tribes really does need to unite. It needs a standing army to defend itself quickly when its land is attacked. And so it makes sense—makes historical sense—for the people to ask for a king; a human approach that might solve both their spiritual and physical needs. But God, instead of saying "Yay" or "Nay," says "Oh dear." And we wonder why?

Kings, of course, bring a whole new realm of problems—conscription, taxation, loss of personal freedoms... And kingdoms aren't the same as tribes. A tribal leader rules *his or her* people wherever they are. But a king rules a land. Suddenly all those non-Israelite neighbors become part of the land, part of Israelite society, and they can't be left out of the laws, people, or nation. Sure, a kingdom means less temptation to intermarry with strangers because there will be no strangers; less temptation to worship other gods because the law of the land will demand you worship one God; less temptation to make your own rules when the nation's rules are enforced. But there's also the danger of corruption from within; and, of course, corruption from on high, should the king chance to fall.

*1 Samuel 13:9, 14:24 describes the beginning of that fall.*

Saul gets impatient when *his* priest fails to arrive on time. He starts by claiming the power of a priest, and ends up making rules that belong to God. Things go wrong (especially for Saul's son Jonathan, already a military hero). Meanwhile, Samuel anoints a young shepherd named David as the next king.

We imagine David soon afterward, still a child, not quite a teenager perhaps, rushing forward to conquer the great Goliath with a simple stone. That's how it looks in Sunday school pictures isn't it? Then our neighbors say *myth* and dismiss the whole Bible. But what if the story in the Bible, as opposed to in tradition, reads like history? What does the Bible really say about David and Goliath?

*1 Samuel 16:18, 18:4 gives a rather different picture of the young man.*

Myth number one is debunked—David is a warrior, not a child, when he fights Goliath; he's similar in his impressive size to the military hero Jonathan who, likewise, is not a small child.

Then there's the whole *giant* Goliath, creature of myth and legend thing…

*2 Samuel 21:15-22 invites us to meet Goliath's brothers.*

Myth number two bites the dust—Goliath is no mythical giant, but a really large man from a tribe of really large men who, not surprisingly, gravitate toward being employed by really large armies.

The Bible says David marries King Saul's daughter, then marries a farmer's widow. He lives in caves and leads the rebels, joins a Philistine tribe, leads a Philistine army, and eventually takes over the Israelite throne on the death of Saul. All of these things are historically convincing. David even heads south to fight the Amalekites when the Philistines launch their final attack on Saul—after all, would you include a *Hebrew* ally in your battle to destroy the *Hebrew* nation, or would you make sure he was seriously busy elsewhere? Even David's multiple marriages make sense—among Middle-Eastern tribes, it's still required that you provide, preferably through marriage, for the widow and children of the man you've killed in battle.

But David didn't take over the throne unopposed. He'd recently been fighting in the south, so he took over the southern tribes (Judah) while Saul's son Ishbosheth took over in the north (otherwise known as Israel). Then Saul's military commander swapped sides, returned David's estranged wife Michal, and was killed for his efforts by David's military commander. What a mess!

*2 Samuel 2:12-16 describes even more mess.*

Even the details of battle, so alien and strange to us, ring true historically. In nomadic hand-to-hand combat, the final stage was to grasp your opponent and deliver a somewhat ritual fatal blow. The mystical twelve (for twelve tribes?) enact that final stage together in *Samuel's* gruesome scene—perhaps a reminder that war isn't glorious and distant; it's dark and personal.

More wars ensue. David conquers Jerusalem—a strategically important location as the priest-king Melchisedek knew so long ago. Joab sneaks through a water-shaft into the city and, again, archeology and history bear witness to the tale. Still fighting against the Philistines (no longer his allies), David engages in a forest battle recalling Greek army techniques as his forces disguise their presence with rustling trees.

*Read 1 Chronicles 14:15 and try to picture it.*

With the Philistines in retreat, David brings the Ark of the Covenant to Jerusalem, thus sealing his power by combining the religious and cultural centers of the nation. (Of course, getting it there is non-trivial, and involves a delay while David learns to respect God's plans rather than his own.) David's long-estranged wife Michal complains when he dances in front of the Ark, a complaint that is probably fueled by rebellion against her lot rather than against God—Michal may be back with her original husband, but she's more like a concubine now, without the privilege due a first-won wife. It's kind of hard (for a woman) not to feel sorry for her.

Soon David defeats the Philistines in the west, the Ammonites in the east, then the Syrians, Moabites and Edomites. He's becoming a major force in the region, but his kingdom won't last long. Sadly this means his presence on the world stage, and in the world's records, is rather small. But the details the Bible gives of David's world are historically convincing.

*Read 2 Samuel 10:4-5. Cutting off someone's beard wasn't just disfiguring; it was a mark of defeat—an appealingly curious historical detail.*

*Read 2 Samuel 12: 27. The capital of the Ammonites was just east of Jerusalem. Archeologists have discovered a huge underground cistern there.*

As David grows older, his sons fight to claim the throne. Bearing in mind the oldest were born to different wives, this isn't too surprising. The most dramatic battle involves Absalom—Amnon rapes Absalom's sister; Absalom has Amnon killed and is banished from court for three years (David doesn't like his sons to kill each other); Absalom returns for two years (David missed him), then insults David's general and grows a political following of his own (oh dear); Absalom declares himself king while his father's still alive. What a serious insult, and threat to national stability!

It's not a pleasant series of stories. We probably won't include the details in a children's storybook. (Let's just stick to the fallen giant… and definitely not the tragic death of Bathsheba's husband). But it's part of the Bible, and it rings historically true. It's part of the story of God's love and mankind's unending mess:

*2 Samuel 15:7 and 1 Kings 2:11 have that number 40 again!*

Some translations say Absalom came back to King David after 40 years. If David reigned 40 years, it would be hard for the battle with Absalom to take a whole 40 years too, but perhaps it was only four years, as other translations suggest. History and common sense play their part, as does interpretation when we read the Bible, as do external resources: Josephus says it was four years.

*2 Samuel 15:19 offers a neat bit of contemporary detail.*

David uses mercenaries in his army, but not just any mercenaries. In particular, he uses soldiers from Gath, the Philistine land where he worked back in *1 Samuel 27:2*. Middle-Eastern armies of the time regularly used mercenaries, so again, the historical details ring true.

Solomon rules as coregent with David towards the end of David's life—a common historical approach (the successor being chosen and groomed by the father). Son Adonijah tries to marry his father's final wife to gain the throne (yes, David had lots of wives). Then on David's death, Solomon makes all the right moves, exiles some, supports others, fulfills obligations etc. He divides the country into 12 provinces, kind of like the United States. He institutes taxation to support the royal household and the army. He makes valuable political alliances.

*1 Kings 3:1 describes one!*

And yes, Solomon even marries the Pharaoh's daughter. He knows how to win friends and influence people! Subsequently, many marriages result in many concubines, a harem such as any influential leader in that age was bound to own. He builds forts. He equips his army with Israel's first war-chariots (chariots at last! *1 Kings 9:19*). He guards those Egyptian and Philistine trade routes through the land of Israel, protects the ports, improves the roads... He builds a Temple, cementing himself as an influence beyond the region and making the most of all David's earlier alliances.

History and (some interpretations of) the Bible disagree when it comes to the date of Solomon's Temple though, which begs the question—will we stick to our favorite Biblical interpretation, or are we free to use other sources to learn what the Bible really means?

*1 Kings 6:1 might be familiar from those numbers in Numbers.*

The Temple is built, and Solomon's reign is established. The boundaries of his kingdom expand...

*1 Kings 9:26-28 shows them expanding to a port on the Red Sea*

... and that Red Sea / Reed Puddle is still a familiar enough place, whatever name it's known by, for Solomon to build his cargo fleet there on the Gulf of Aqaba.

*1 Kings 10:1-2 reveals the nation's spreading influence.*

A queen comes to visit Solomon and gives gifts, probably as part of a trade agreement. Perhaps we'll find her bank statements one day, because writing has become more important—keeping historical records, writing inspirational words, setting out rules and regulations... Not all things written will survive, of course, but many are copied out over and over again until the days when some precious copies survive.

David wrote psalms. Solomon wrote proverbs, songs and more. Both kings were part of the educated elite in Israel. David's psalms often refer to relevant places, enemies and customs, as do Solomon's writings. Ideas from neighboring regions find their way into the books, because David and Solomon were surely readers as well. Meanwhile, prophets and historians wrote documents which would be combined, by different groups and cliques, into familiar books of the Bible. Priestly supporters will write Chronicles, emphasizing law and ritual; those looking for salvation from a king will compile the books of Kings—hence a frequent overlap in words with different emphases in the two books.

But time passed and this great Solomon, universally revered, fell out of favor with God. The temptations of the world (*1 Kings 11:*3) proved too much for the man of wisdom. On his death, the throne passed to a son who refused to listen to the wise advice of old men, and the country split in two again—Israel and Judah just like when David first came to power.

The historical story continues in *Kings* and *Chronicles*, confirmed by other historical documents and archeological discoveries which reveal…

- ivory inlays in the furniture of the rich (as condemned by Amos);
- King Ahab bringing 10,000 infantry and 2,000 chariots to the battle of Qarqar;
- King Mesha of Moab rebelling against Israel in the 9th century BC;
- King Jehu of Israel kissing Chalmaneser's feet on the Black Obelisk;
- Judah leading a revolt against Assyria;
- Tiglath-Pielser III laying waste to cities and conquering Galilee, deporting the Jewish population;
- the broad wall of King Hezekiah, built to enlarge Jerusalem when refugees arrived from Israel;
- Hezekiah's water tunnel;
- images of the destruction of Lachish;

- Babylonian arrow-heads in homes destroyed by fire in Jerusalem;
- the seal of Governor Gedaliah; and more.

You can find all these stories if you look for them in the Bible, and all these verifications in the world's museums.

If the Bible gets these historical details so convincingly right, isn't that a good argument for suggesting that it just might get the God stuff right as well? History as a path or an anchor to faith? And if the history is so frequently verified, isn't that a good reason to reconsider our interpretation of the Bible, instead of arguing? Perhaps it's even a good reason to let our children and neighbors ask questions. But more importantly, it might suggest a good argument for keeping our minds guardedly open to *whatever* channel God uses to speak to us and our children. Let's check the Bible against the *facts*, and check facts against the Bible, in the knowledge that truth lies somewhere between discovery and interpretation—and in the knowledge that the Holy Spirit, author of the Bible, will surely guide us.

> *To learn more about how Bible events fit into the history of the times, read the notes and tables in* the NKJV Chronological Study Bible.

# Faith and Politics: Kings and Chronicles

Ah, but those kings had so many shifting alliances… which leads to two things we should never talk about around the dinner table: faith and politics. (Death and taxes aren't recommended either; but perhaps they're just the same thing under different names.)

When I was a kid, our family faith was shared (apart from the whole Catholic-Methodist thing). Which just left politics for the rebellious teen. And in my case, that rebel was Big Brother; he argued politics every Saturday lunchtime with Dad. It was enough to put me off the subject for life. But it wasn't enough to stop me (sort of) making up my own mind when I grew old enough to vote. By coincidence, my own mind was the same as my parents', but we lived in a three-party society at the time, so my vote was bracketed (and presumably cancelled out) by one brother voting to the left of me and the other to the right.

Big Brother didn't eat lunch with us anymore, and he'd grown up. He didn't even argue with Dad, and neither did we. Because somewhere along the line we'd learned that what mattered was knowing we all shared the same real values. No (human) political party was going to fix everything. No (human) political ideology would be devoid of flaws. And politics was just a choice of pilot for a ship lost at sea—only faith would find the way.

What if we hadn't learned? What if we were still arguing, all the way until my dad died? Would we have grown each more committed to our own political choice, until we forgot the values that helped us make that choice—until we forgot that our siblings shared those same values and treasured them just as surely as ourselves? Would we have put up so many defenses that we ended up believing politics could save us—and the wrong politics condemn?

My kids don't all share my politics, but that's okay. My neighbors don't either, or my friends. And sometimes I want—oh how I want—to argue that Christians ought to agree with *me*… but they probably shouldn't. There can't be only one way for "real" Christians to vote—because different political formulae get different things right and wrong. There can't be only one political party that God can approve. (What if there's none?) And we really can't put our faith in politics instead of in God.

The kings of God's people were certainly politicians, though it's not clear which party would love them most. King Solomon, following his father, David, was a master of political alliances and destructions. Of course, Solomon served as co-regent with David for many years before becoming king—he had his chance to learn the ropes. On David's death, he promptly got rid of any opposition that might take advantage of a change of leadership. He killed the brother who was most conspicuously conspiring against him (*just let me marry Daddy's concubine*); exiled the priest who switched sides on his father; killed the manipulative general Joab who might have tried to seize the throne; executed a long-term, frequently pardoned enemy Shimei (*1 Kings 2*)... etc. But Solomon's son, Rehoboam, didn't have the privilege of a long co-regency... which might explain his youthful arrogance and political naïveté, resulting in the loss of half the kingdom.

In spiritual terms, Rehoboam lost half the kingdom because of his father's faithlessness. Which puts faith and politics very firmly on the same page. It kind of begs the question though, what was wrong with Solomon's faith. He started out great and wasn't condemned for his alliances with non-believing nations, so that wasn't it. He gathered resources from far and wide in his efforts to build God's Temple; God didn't reject the gifts. Cosmopolitan Judea must have harbored many foreigners who didn't follow God's law, but Solomon wasn't ordered to murder them, so that wasn't the problem. What went wrong?

Solomon's wives, by definition, represented the king's political prowess, and God never condemned him (as far as the Bible tells us) for *marrying* them. God didn't even condemn Solomon for letting his wives worship their own gods—in God's own land! But God *did* condemn Solomon for worshipping the gods of his wives. Marriage was acceptable politics, but worship is faith, and the two are not the same.

*1 Kings 11:9-10 describes why God is angry. Verses 31-32 describe what will happen next.*

The prophet Ahijah gives ten twelfths of a robe to the leader of Solomon's army, showing how ten of the twelve tribes will be lost. Of course, it's not entirely clear which ten (or why 10+1=12—there are lots of theories). But now, Rehoboam will keep just Judah and Simeon (though Simeon's not technically a tribe at all, and is totally enclosed by Judah). The border tribes (two tribes perhaps) of Benjamin will keep changing sides in the middle, while the Levites will be permanently scattered since they were never given any land. Counting to twelve tribes becomes seriously complicated, but counting to two, two countries, isn't so hard.

Two countries and two political parties perhaps? They certainly had two very different ways of going about things, and, contrary to tradition, they were both loved by God.

Jeroboam, still a loyal subject of Solomon, flees to Egypt, which is still a political ally bound by marriage. When Solomon dies, Jeroboam returns to his homeland and leads a delegation to the new king, Rehoboam, demanding reduced taxes—ah, what a political livewire. Young King Rehoboam rejects the advice of his elders—new leader wielding a *new broom* perhaps. He needs those taxes to keep up the royal palaces, fund Temple worship, and pay the soldiers who serve in his armies.

*1 Kings 12:1-8 gives a very timely tale of political folly.*

So Jeroboam leads a political revolt, and the country splits.

**WHAT HAPPENS IN THE NORTH?**

Jeroboam's revolt leads to a major religious problem for God's people. There are Levites in the north, but the Temple is in the south. If people go home to the Temple in Jerusalem to worship, they'll likely end up undermining the northern king's authority. So politics demand a solution. Jeroboam calls for a return to *traditional* worship of God on the high places—and of course, there was nothing wrong with that in the old days, only two generations ago, as long as God's name wasn't profaned with the names of other gods.

Turning the whole country, symbolically, into a temple, Jeroboam replaces the oxen who carry the Temple's *golden sea* (a large water bowl in Jerusalem) with two calves carrying the country at its border. Of course, given the whole golden calf episode, it's not hard to see why some thought this heretical. The Biblical record declares

Jeroboam has created new *gods*, whether or not that was his intent—history, even Biblical history, being written by the victors of course. And some, though not all, of God's priestly Levites flee south.

*In 2 Chronicles 11:14, written from a priestly perspective, it sounds like they all fled, though Ezekiel 44:10 suggests quite a number remained.*

So how does God feel about all this politics? Stories of the prophets in Israel make it clear God didn't reject his people, nor did He leave them without holy priests. But the return of the most fervent priests to Judah might have led to a Temple-based priesthood, more devoted to ritual than ever before, after such exposure to ritual decay. These priests and their followers soon start compiling historical documents into the book of *Chronicles*, adding their priestly (and possibly political) slant to the tale.

God promised David that his line would last forever. But no such promises were made to Jeroboam by the prophet. Jeroboam's son takes the throne after his father, but is killed in a palace coup by Baasha, thus ending his line. Baasha's son Elah takes over after him and probably dies in another coup. Zimri, a military leader, holds the throne for a whole seven days, but Omri and Tibni fight to claim it from him. Omri wins and becomes so famous his name is included on a Moabite monument, though he scarcely merits a paragraph in the Bible. (Maybe that says something about how God looks on political power—and maybe that's something to remember when we're tempted to raise politics to the level of faith.)

Omri builds Samaria into the new grand capital of Israel, and his son Ahab marries the very famous Jezebel—a Zidonian / Pheonician princess and much hated Biblical antagonist... Besides her famously anti-God stance, she's also important politically, a stabilizing force protecting Israel on the world stage.

All this happens in the northern kingdom of Israel, a land that borders Syria via Damascus. Ben-Hadad of Syria sends armies south to invade as Syria expands. Then God helps Ahab, for all that Ahab's a bad guy, proving God is God of His people in the hills and on the plains, and also proving God's help doesn't imply God's political approval—a lesson modern day maneuverers might do well to remember. Ahab later makes a treaty with Syria and is condemned by the prophet Elijah. But the land remains free.

Ahab's son Ahaziah dies soon after gaining the throne, but the royal line survives and Ahaziah's brother Jehoram takes his place. Meanwhile, the Moabites, sensing weakness, invade from the east. Jehoram calls on his traditional enemies, Judah and Edom, to help. It's a strange combination of armies, which results in a Moabite defeat, probably due to overconfidence. Judah and Israel end up on such good terms that King Ahaziah of Judah marries Athaliah, sister of Ahab, therefore aunt to King Jehoram of Israel. The tradition of political marriages continues to grow strong, though it's not clear that God approves this time. Eventually Elishah (successor to Elijah) starts another rebellion by talking with the warrior Jehu.

*2 Kings 9:1-10 show that, yes, prophets do affect politics, and so does faith! But perhaps not the way we expected*

Jehoram of Israel and Ahaziah of Judah both die in the subsequent battles—dying for the sin of trusting in politics instead of in God perhaps, and killed in battle as leaders often were.

**MEANWHILE, IN THE SOUTH...**

History in the south hasn't gone much better by this time, for all that we're taught to view Israel as bad and Judah as good. Rehoboam fails to defend against Shishak of Egypt and loses the Temple treasures—God's riches for man's politics? He replaces them with fakes in a politically savvy move that's not terribly faithful to God.

*Read 1 Kings 14:26-27 to find some Biblical counterfeits!*

Rehoboam's son Abijam inherits the throne and continues to oppose Jeroboam in Israel while failing to obey God in Judah... Ah how easily we spot the plank in our neighbor's eye! David's line is safe, but its faithfulness is seriously in question.

Abijam's son Asa reigns after him, bringing the nation back to God. *Hurray*! Then Ethiopia invades. Judah wins. *Hurray again*! And the border tribes of Benjamin join with Judah—it was tough living on a border, even then.

King Baasha of Israel (leader of that palace coup against Jeroboam's son) invades Judah in an attempt to reclaim Banjamin's land. He builds a border fortress at Ramah, at which point King Asa of Judah asks the Syrians to help (can help really come from God's enemies?). Asa pays them, no surprise, with the remaining Temple treasures—it's sensible politics, but not very faith-filled, again, and he loses God's favor.

*2 Chronicles 16:1-3 gives a fine picture of political machinations.*

Ben-Hadad of Syria has already conquered Damascus at this time. Asking his aid is a good political move for King Asa, though future prophets will soon condemn human alliances with faithless neighbors. When Ben-Hadad attacks in the north of Israel, the Israelite troops, engaged in enlarging Israel's borders at Ramah, are swiftly reassigned. Then Israel fights Ben-Hadad in the north, leaving Judah free to regain and reinforce its border towns.

The prophet Hanani speaks out against King Asa for trusting in God's enemies. Hanani is put in jail, at which point Asa becomes ill for the rest of his life. Refusing to listen to advice was a problem them, just as it is today. So was giving unpopular advice—tough to be a prophet or politician.

Jehoshaphat, son of Asa, tries to redeem the land from foreign alliances by joining Ahab of Israel in the war against Syria. But the alliance fails, as prophesied by the Israelite prophet Macaiah, and denied by the *false* prophet Zedekiah.

*1 Kings 22:7-17 describes the competing prophecies.*

Clearly God still had prophets (true prophets like Macaiah) on both sides of the border. God is still God of Israel as well as Judah after all. (And we might be surprised which nations today prove to have God on their side.)

More border battles ensue between Judah and the Ammonites (in the south) and Moabites (in the east). Then Jehoshaphat allies with Ahab's son Ahaziah and the Edomites in that famously unexpected battle against the Moabites. Jehoshaphat's son, Jehoram, marries Ahab's daughter—a political move that might cement relations but won't please God. Then Jehoram and Ahaziah both die in battle.

## BACK IN THE NORTH...

Jehoram's son, King Ahaziah of Judah (perhaps named for his uncle in Israel), joins Ahaziah's brother, King Joram of Israel, in fighting Syria again—this on the death of their one-time ally Ben-Hadad, as prophesied by Elisha. Then Elisha, the political prophet, anoints Jehu, who starts his reign in Israel with a house-cleaning killing spree. He kills King Joram of Israel (thus gaining the throne), kills King Ahaziah of Judah (thus breaking the alliance—no surprise), kills all of Israel's royal family (including Jezebel, thus breaking the alliance with Pheonicia), and proceeds to murder hundreds of others. It's a massacre still denounced a hundred years later by the prophet Hosea, and it leaves Israel seriously vulnerable to Syria and Assyria.

*Hosea 1:4 shows Hosea prophesying the end of Jehu's line.*

Which all begs the question, was Jehu chosen because he would kill so many; did he kill because he wanted more power than he'd been given; was he chosen to punish? Military and political success don't mean (and won't mean) the same as God's favor, however much we might want to claim they do.

Jehu's successor, King Jehoahaz of Israel, prays for relief from Syria and gets it when Hazael is succeeded by another Ben-Hadad. (Names are inherited as well as titles, which might explain why the king's names are so hard to keep apart in the Bible.) Jehoahaz' son Jehoash becomes king of Israel and asks the now elderly Elisha for help, resulting in a prophesy about Israel being saved three times from Syria (*2 Kings 13:14-19*). Jeroboam (another Jeroboam—remember those inherited names) climbs to the throne after Jehoash, his father, dies. And Israel thrives, regaining territory in both north and south. A golden era begins, but it won't last.

The fall begins with God's surprising love for His people's enemies. At this point Assyria is rising in power, and God really seems to care about their welfare! He sends Jonah, the new prophet in Jeroboam's court, to save the Assyrian capital, Nineveh. Meanwhile, Amos and Hosea warn Israel.

*Read Jonah 4:2, Amos 3:1, 9:7. Both cases show that God blesses nations, regardless of whether they* belong *to him.*

The intrigue continues when Jeroboam's son Zecharaiah is assassinated by Shallum, who's assassinated by Menahem. Menahem rules 10 years, followed by his son Pekahiah, who is assassinated by the anti-Assyrian Pekah. Israel and Syria combine forces to attack Judah, hoping to force the southern nation into an anti-Assyrian alliance. But Hoshea assassinates Pekah and bows to

Assyrian rule after all, then falls after seeking an alternative alliance with Egypt. And thus, Israel is lost.

If the politics of alliance and assassination sounds similar to the present day, perhaps there's a reason for that. Way back when Solomon was king, he wrote that there's "no new thing under the sun," and it's still true (*Ecclesiastes 1:9*).

## MEANWHILE IN JUDAH (the south)...

Do you remember when Jehu killed Ahaziah of Judah and Joram of Israel in that mighty killing spree? Ahaziah's mother, the daughter of the infamous Jezebel, tries to take Judah's throne at this point. But the youngest son and heir, Joash, survives her murderous attempt. Joash comes to the throne and revives the Temple and Temple taxes (faith and politics again), but ends up handing the Temple gold over to Hazael of Damascus (and Syria).

*2 Kings 12:1-18 gives a vivid picture of taxation, due diligence and corruption before Joash is killed.*

When Joash is murdered (after falling out with the priests) his son Amaziah takes the throne. He quells an Edomite invasion, and hires—then fires—mercenaries from Israel. Firing them is a politically risky move, of course, resulting in war with Israel, again.

Amaziah loses to Jehoash during Israel's golden era. Uzziah, Amaziah's son, becomes king after him, at which time the prophet Isaiah appears in Judah, echoing the prophecies of Amos and Hosea in Israel. Uzziah successfully fights the Philistines in the west, using new *long-range weapons* (ah, technology!). But he makes the same mistake as that first King Saul (believing he can burn incense before the Lord just as well as any priest), so he gets sick (leprosy) and his son Jotham rules as co-regent during his isolation.

*Read 2 Chronicles 26:19-21. At least Jotham had the chance to learn politics from Dad before inheriting the throne!*

When Israel allies with Syria *against* Assyria, Judah makes a political alliance *with* Assyria instead. When Pekah attacks to annex Judah and force her help in the war, Jotham's son Ahaz buys Assyria's aid with Temple gold, yet again. God makes the famous promise, through the prophet Isaiah, of a virgin conceiving a child—a promise fulfilled when Pekah's threat recedes in the time it would take for a child to grow. Of course, like all prophecy, it's a promise containing a message for the future too.

Israel's population (or at least, its power-base) has been exiled by Syria now. The northern land is settled by foreigners and survivors, but still keeps a Jewish priesthood, permitted in order to *placate* the God of Israel (because gods were believed to belong to places, not people). Israel still harbors prophets as well, who wander the countryside. Meanwhile in Judah, Ahaz' son Hezekiah gains the throne, writes more proverbs (*Proverbs 25:1*), and tries to reunite the two countries against Assyria. When he falls ill, the king of Babylon (very subtly) sends an envoy to enquire after his health (and spy out the land). Isaiah prophesies that Babylon will conquer Judah after Hezekiah's death.

Sennacherib of Assyria is on the move. He conquers large parts of Judah, refusing to be deterred by tributes of remaining Temple gold. But Tirhakah of Ethiopia heads north from Egypt, and Sennacherib's army retreats. Did Egypt save Judah, or did God? Faith *or* politics?

Manasseh becomes king after Hezekiah, but he is captured and taken to Babylon. His son Amon is assassinated, and Amon's son Josiah takes the throne. Aged only eight, Josiah is proclaimed as the *good king*, the one who might restore God's kingdom. Perhaps there's some blend of King and Messiah in the people's hopes. And perhaps we too like to blend our kings / presidents / governors and messiahs, our faith and our politics.

*2 Kings 23:25 ends a chapter of praise for the young king's holiness, but the story swiftly turns around in verse 29.*

The people put their trust in kings (or presidents, or parties). Kings trust political alliances and social manipulation. Politicians make what they think are the best choices, and deride those prophets (or pundits) who say their choices are wrong. Soon the offices of politician and prophet are hopelessly intertwined. False prophets (purveyors of fake news) declare peace where there is none, true prophets flee heresy (and ejection from the party). And today…?

But how could those kings have known the right way to go (and how can we know)? It's easy, with hindsight, to declare certain prophets to be false, yes-men, self-serving even, but they probably thought they were well-educated, well-versed in the ways of the world, and well-trained in serving God. And the king simply had advisors—no certainty about the future for him.

The prophet Jeremiah will soon tell his king that God's people are bound to be defeated, carried off into captivity. No policies (or politics) will save them if he's to be believed, so what's a king to do? This king screams in fury and has the prophet thrown in jail (or worse). But does his error lie in not obeying Jeremiah, or in deriding him so loudly that no one can hear God's "small voice"?

Is *our* error more likely to lie in not voting for the right political party, or in deriding our opponents so loudly that no one around us can hear God's small voice?

## SO, WAS JOSIAH A MESSIAH?

With young King Josiah eager to please God, the priest Hilkiah, perhaps seeking to escape past politics, *discovers* the book of God's law hidden in the Temple (*Ah... but who hid it?*). During Josiah's short reign, Temple worship is restored, priests and prophets, including Zephaniah, preach reform and speak out against those countries Judah has trusted for political aid, *Trust in the Lord* is the call—and God wins... except Josiah dies too young, and Jeremiah (whose friend, Baruch, may have had much to do with the rediscovery of documents in the Temple) has much to tell (and much to suffer too).

Judah really is about to be taken into captivity, and Jeremiah knows it. The Promised Land will be left without God's people, and the future of this clever, blessed, small but influential and sacred nation will hang in the balance.

The Bible tells a vivid and genuine tale of history of politics. It even tells us about what matters more than politics. But it doesn't tell us which way to vote in the next election. It doesn't tell politicians how to prioritize between interpretations of God's law. And it certainly doesn't give us a blueprint for our children's or our neighbors' political leanings. But it does remind us to trust God, pray to God, and remember that God is in control.

> *The* IVP Atlas of the Bible *does a great job putting those shifting alliances of Israel and Judah into perspective.*

# Faith and Mystery: Jeremiah and Deuteronomy

Some people search the Bible for mysteries. They make movies where dangerous treasures have magical powers. They write books about secret codes and hidden messages. They cling to coincidence, symbol and sign, ignoring message and design. Then our kids subscribe solely to mystery and mystique, where Disneyesque legends offer valiant monsters for good guys to seek and destroy. Until they grow up and reject it all as fantasy and dream.

Does that mean we should never look to solve mysteries in the Bible? Will all investigation lead us into fiction and heresy? Our questions—our growing children's questions—might lead us away from some beloved interpretations; that's for sure. But God is bigger than all our questions. God's word can stand up to closer inspection. And the solutions just might lead us closer to God, if we trust Him enough to look for them.

That prophet, Jeremiah, is important to one of my favorite mysteries: Why are the books of Jeremiah and Deuteronomy—so far apart in the Bible—so similar in words; why does Deuteronomy even exist when it's little more than a repeat of the first four books, and what's the answer to that vexed question of who wrote the Pentateuch. (Did Moses really write the story of his own death? And did God dictate creation to him, or did Moses hear that tale at his real mother's knee, then write it on his stepmother's papyrus notepaper? And did someone else...?)

The first people to study these questions weren't trying to undermine the Bible, despite the reputation that modern complaint might ascribe to them—they were Biblical scholars seeking to learn and understand more from God's word. Their conclusions, though they may challenge that idea of an ancient Moses describing his own death, don't contradict any Biblical message—just the traditions or translations we love to adhere to. Perhaps more authors than Moses had a hand in those first five books. Maybe someone else edited Moses' text (besides Joshua transcribing it in *Joshua 8:32*). Then different groups might have maintained the same stories around campfires, until writing (preservable writing) was established in the tribe. Different tribes could each have carried their own documents. And so, when the stories were combined, we end up with slightly different versions written in the same Bible (two creation stories in *Genesis 1* and *2* for example; two lists of how many animals went into the ark...).

Researchers began identifying different authors for those first five books as long ago as the 1800s. They examined the different phrasing in repeated stories, and different names (Yahweh and El) for God. Like peering onto the backside of a tapestry, they identified threads of different colors, or authors, characterized as below:

- *E* always speaks of God as El or Elohim, but doesn't particularly emphasize the duties of priests.
- *P* also speaks of El, but is deeply concerned with priestly ritual.
- *J* refers to God as Yahweh (or Jehovah)
- And *D* is the author of Deuteronomy (which you will probably have noticed, retells a lot of Moses' story almost from scratch, in the form of the great man's last sermon).

Ah, but who is *D*, and why did *D* feel the need to re-record the tale already told?

*J* and *E* are assumed to have come from Judah and Israel respectively, the latter perhaps bearing documents that were taken to Israel (or left there) when the countries split. For example, the delightfully unpleasant story of Jacob's sons massacring Diana's lover and his tribe to conquer Shechem (*Genesis 34*) is rewritten in the much pleasanter claim that the town was purchased just before in *Genesis 33:18-20*—the first (gentle) story corresponds to *E*, treasured perhaps in Israel, where Shechem became a holy city; the second (violent) tale corresponds to *J*, beloved in Judah and emphasizing the depravation associated with the northern kingdom's holy city. But how did the different writings (or collections) come to be reunited into the Pentateuch—a collection of books that appear on the surface to have one author, unlike the New Testament gospels, which never pretended to anything other than four?

After the fall of Israel, when refugees (including priests) flooded back into Judea, the priests in the Temple would be highly motivated to reunite the religion, people and tribes. Collecting and compiling surviving books from both sides would make a good start, and God's inspiration would guide them as they stitched the accounts back together—nothing lost, nothing left out, even nothing glossed over because this was, after all, God's sacred word.

But the people continued to rebel against God, just as before. They continued to sacrifice meat in their homes (ah, dinner!) and on the high places, while priests insisted all sacrifice must take place in God's Temple. They continued to worship in their own way, scattered, separate—Israelites who hadn't darkened the Temple doors in years, with lapsed Judeans happily following them. King Hezekiah introduced reforms, but they didn't stick. Then young Josiah came to the throne. And then a new book was *found*.

King Hezekiah must surely have had access to the holy books of God's word. So what did the priest Hilkiah find hidden in the Temple (*2 Kings 22:8*)? What did Josiah read that so prompted his greater reforms?

Tradition has long suggested Hilkiah and Shaphan discovered the book of *Deuteronomy*. Meanwhile, linguistic scholars (and curious readers) have long been convinced that Deuteronomy was written by a different author from the other four books in the Pentateuch. Deuteronomy does indeed include some stricter codes. *Deuteronomy 12:1-7* requires the people to destroy all the high places of worship, and worship God only at the one place of His choosing, presumably His Temple. But Samuel sacrificed and worshiped in many high places without condemnation... *Deuteronomy 17:14-20* offers laws for *good kings*, even though the Israelite tribes had no desire for kings in Moses' day. Curious readers wonder why.

Deuteronomy's priestly laws and royal injunctions fit well with Josiah's strict reforms... and with the needs (national, cultural and spiritual) of a divided people attempting to reunite under one God. But that still leaves the question of who wrote the book. It's a mystery, for those who like mysteries. For those who don't, it's a side-issue taking nothing from the fact that God is the ultimate author, inspirer and director of our faith. God inspired the writers, whether Moses or *E*, *P*, *J* or *D*. God directed the people. And God is sovereign over the preceding and ensuing history.

The Bible's mystery is a side-issue, if you like, that should not cause us to argue, rebuke, deny, or otherwise turn inquirers away from our faith. Those inquiring into it will have to look deeply at the word of God, and God himself has promised to speak through His word. So let's not turn those seekers of mystery away, be they authors of fiction or students of history. Instead let's ask, with them, who might D have been?

Richard Elliott Friedman offers an intriguing analysis in *Who Wrote the Bible?* suggesting that Jeremiah the prophet may have compiled those ancient writings into a new book. But what would be Jeremiah's connection with this?

- Jeremiah began his prophetic ministry during King Josiah's reign, even composing a lamentation for Josiah when he died (*2 Chronicles 35:25*).
- Jeremiah was closely connected with Hilkiah and Shaphan, later sending letters to the Babylonian exiles by the hands of their sons (*Jeremiah 29:1-3*).
- Shaphan's sons heard Jeremiah's prophecies in the court of Josiah's son Jehoiakim (*Jeremiah 36:10*), saved him from being stoned (*Jeremiah 26:24*), and provided him refuge when Nebuchadnezzar took control of the country (*Jeremiah 39:14, 40:5-6*).

Jeremiah was clearly scholarly, a great thinker, pray-er and writer, and deeply devoted to God, even to the extent of risking his life over and again in God's service. He appears to be a priest from the priestly school of Shiloh, which was hugely important in the reformation. And if reform were truly in the air, he would have been a great candidate to lead the charge. But these aren't the only connections between Jeremiah and Deuteronomy. Even the words and phrasings feel the same (similar in translation might not mean much, but similar in the original language means a lot):

- *Deuteronomy 28:1* and *Jeremiah 17:24* both describe what will be if we "diligently" listen to Yahweh's voice.
- *Deuteronomy 10:16* and *Jeremiah 4:4* both refer to circumcision of the "foreskin of your heart" rather than the flesh (a concept echoed in the New Testament).
- *Deuteronomy 4:19* and *Jeremiah 8:2, Deuteronomy 17:3* and *Jeremiah 19:13* all refer to the "host of the heaven."
- *Deuteronomy 4:20* and *Jeremiah 11:4* both refer to Egypt as "the iron furnace."

- *Deuteronomy 4:29, 10:12, 11:13 and 13:14* and *Jeremiah 32:41* all include reference to hearts and souls.
- *Deuteronomy 4:26* and *Jeremiah 22:26* both refer to exile.

None of this means the mystery is solved of course. Friedmann goes further to suggest Jeremiah was instrumental in collecting (collating and compiling—even writing) many other books of Old Testament history, sculpting the story to emphasize the importance of priests and kings, and the coming of a king who would redeem the land—the Messiah perhaps… or Josiah until, sadly, he got himself killed. After the king's death, Jeremiah might have tried to reshape his message, emphasizing exile as a part of God's plan. Alternatively, after the king's death, God would have inspired Jeremiah to revisit his message, emphasizing exile as a part of God's plan.

*Read 2 Kings 23:21-25 and contrast the triumphal tone with what follows in 2 Kings 23:26-27. There is a suggestion that "neither after him arose there any like him" could have been added later when the young king died.*

And so Friedmann offers a solution to the *mystery*. We don't have to believe him. But the difference between faith and denial doesn't lie in our willingness to question or to avoid questions, but rather in our willingness to listen to that *still small voice* and know the author is guiding us as we read. We can listen, and while listening we can delight in the mystery. Our children can question, and while looking for answers can hear God's small voice, unless we drown it out with our complaint.

So yes, there are mysteries in the Bible, and we can use human tools to look for answers. Should we make rules to forbid the use of those tools, because they're not Biblical?

*Matthew 15:9 seems to offer a low opinion of human rules*

Let's teach and study and learn what the Bible says, and be careful not to turn it into what we think it says.

*To learn more theories about how the Bible text was written into human words, read Richard Elliott Friedman's excellent book,* Who Wrote The Bible?

# Faith and the Supernatural: Elijah, Elisha, Isaiah, Daniel and Revelation

There are lots of people with supernatural skill in the Bible, visionaries describing the future, sages rife with spiritual advice, and even wandering foreigners who talk to donkeys (*Numbers 22:21-35*). There are lots of warnings against unbiblical spiritual practices too. And we're wise to heed those warnings, but how far should we take them? What happens when we try to apply them to our neighbors?

If Biblical prophets and prophecies are real, is it wrong to read a horoscope? If horoscopes are okay, is it wrong to consult a medium? If end-times fiction is okay, should we forbid the reading of young-adult dystopias? Stories about magicians? Talking animals? And where do computer games, meditation, and tales of magic and monsters fit into it all? How we strain to know the rules!

And, come to that, where does prayer for guidance fit in, if we shouldn't try to see into the future? (Yes, I have really heard that question.)

It's easy to see our own faith's rules as simple; easy to point indignantly at those who disobey our interpretation of what's allowed. But sometimes we need to be reminded how easily others might view *us* as deceived. (And really, would you believe a story about a talking donkey if it wasn't in the Bible?)

Elijah and Elisha lived in the early days of kingdoms. Elijah, followed by Elisha, condemned the following of false gods and spoke the true God's words to kings and citizens. They also performed some rather odd supernatural deeds:

- Creating rain and drought (*1 Kings 17:1, 18:45*)
- Creating an infinite supply of oil (*1 Kings 17:14, 2 Kings 4:4*)
- Raising the dead (*1 Kings 17:22, 2 Kings 4:34, 13:21*)
- Prophesying unpleasant deaths, famines, and more (*1 Kings 21:23, 2 Kings 7:1, 8:1,10,12, 9:7, 13:17,19*)
- Setting fire to soldiers (*2 Kings 1:10*)

- Parting rivers—ah, we've seen that one before (*2 Kings 2:8,14*)
- Healing poison (*2 Kings 4:41*)
- Feeding the five thousand—well, maybe not quite 5,000 (*2 Kings 4:43*)
- Healing and causing sickness (*2 Kings 5:14,27*)
- Knowing hidden things (*2 Kings 5:26, 6:9*)
- Floating axe heads (*2 Kings 6:6*)
- Blinding and healing soldiers (*2 Kings 6:18,20*)

Would you accept these as suitable reading if they were in a novel? In a computer game?

Elijah and Elisha are remembered most as prophets of course. And Isaiah is another great prophet, entering the story somewhat later, and well-known today to believers and unbelievers alike. Isaiah's writings start in the time of King Uzziah and might, depending on which tradition we prefer, continue all the way into exile and return... which would make him *fairly old* by the standards of the time.

Would you believe a story about a man who lived multiple generations if it wasn't in the Bible? Would it be heretical to look for an alternative explanation? Maybe Isaiah only *seems* old because he prophecies the future from way in the past—then died at a normal age. God could easily have told him the name of King Cyrus—Isaiah doesn't have to lived in Cyrus' time. But why would God bother to tell him a distant king's name? Alternatively, a later transcriber might have inserted Cyrus' name when he appeared so obviously in Isaiah's book... Or...

Isaiah is one of the greatest (surely most famous) prophets of the birth of Christ (assuming we adhere to Christian interpretation). But followers of other traditions interpret his words very faithfully, and differently. What *we* see clearly might not be clear at all to someone else, and witnessing that it's *obvious* probably won't help.

Jeremiah is another great and famous prophet—wholly Biblical and Biblically holy. He was consulted by kings who needed guidance in a changing world as Babylon arose. He's the one who reminded priests and royals that exile was inevitable. He begged governments not to trust in political alliances, then he mourned when Jerusalem burned. Jeremiah continued to mourn when lessons weren't learned. Jeremiah is surely a great prophet for today, in a world of shifting politics and faiths.

Then there's Ezekiel who saw chariots of fire, wheels within wheels, and monsters with impossible features. Meanwhile Daniel, a prophet at the same time, saw statues made of stone and gold, and prophesied horns that rise up and destroy other horns, and an "abomination that maketh desolate" in the Temple. What do we make of them? And how do we distinguish between Daniel's curious visions and the fictions of today's computer games?

If we say these things are okay as long as God is telling the story, will that help us recognize God? How do we know if it's okay to give half our fortune to a TV medium if he says he's a Christian? To passionately follow end-times horror if the author goes to church? Or instead... to keep our children from watching scary movies until they leave home and watch them without us?

The Bible really does set some clear ground rules in *Leviticus 19:31, Deuteronomy 13:1-3,* and *Isaiah 8:19-20,* though our skeptical children and neighbors might justifiably ask *how clear is clear*?

- No consulting mediums:
    - But Saul consulted the Witch of Endor, and God granted him an answer from Samuel (*1 Samuel 28:8-14*). Of course, Saul died soon afterward, perhaps being punished for his crime.
    - Meanwhile Paul made the medium fall silent in *Acts 16:16-19*
- No chasing after "spirits" (ghosts in other translations):
    - But the disciples believed ghosts might still appear to them (*Matthew 14:25-27, Luke 24:37-39*)
    - And ghosts walked the streets at Jesus' death (*Matthew 27:52-53*)
- No asking others what the future will bring:
    - But asking prophets seems to be okay, as long as the prophets are true. The Bible tell stories of false prophets giving false advice of course (*Ezekiel 13:2-7*), so how can we tell?

The modern world has a fondness for angels, and they're surely scriptural. But why might a fictional TV series about angels be okay, when one about wounded people needing divine assistance to fight demons gets banned?

Spirit guides are a part of America's modern culture. Are they angels when they're good and demons when bad? Do they fit into our Biblical worldview? And what about the blessings of loved ones reappearing after death (something that many bereaved and believing Christians will attest to, and many non-believers also enjoy on television)? What about preparing for the ending of time and calculating the date? Reading end-times novels, or teen dystopias? What about…?

The Bible gives an answer. "Seek ye first the kingdom of God," we're told in *Matthew 6:33*, "…and all these things shall be added unto you." But seeking prophecies of the future, born of longing to know and needing to control, is a very human desire as well as a divinely answered one. So where might we draw the line between divine and dangerous?

Isaiah begins his ministry during the reign of King Uzziah of Judah and continues to prophesy through the reigns of Jotham, Ahaz, and Hezekiah (*Isaiah 1:1*)—quite probably during the reign of Manasseh too. (According to some traditions, Isaiah was chopped in two by order of Manasseh, who might have been his grandson!) Isaiah was married, perhaps to another prophet (*Isaiah 8:3*), had two sons with names whose translations mean "spoil quickly, plunder easily"—which the kingdom did indeed fall prey to—and "a remnant shall return" (*Isaiah 7:3*)—which it did, of course. The second son was born during the reign of King Ahaz, at a time when Shalmanezer was threatening to conquer Judah.

> *In Isaiah 7:14-17, the* virgin *of Christian tradition is interpreted simply as a young woman in other traditions. And the time between a child's conception and adulthood is how long the trials will continue.*

Some interpretations suggest that Isaiah's second son, conceived immediately after this prophecy, was the immediate fulfilment—but prophecies are frequently three-fold, holding meaning for the immediate hearer, hearers throughout time, and future hearers as well. So how will we answer when a neighbor suggests the virgin wasn't Mary? Our immediate instinct, to disagree, disavows the prophecy's first meaning. Is it possible that a qualified agreement with the neighbor, instead, might encourage them to read further in the Bible? Which would we prefer?

*When you read Isaiah 38:1-8, if you try hard enough, you might think of a natural explanation for the sun "returned ten degrees." But it's hard to find natural explanations for how Isaiah knew the king would live fifteen years longer.*

Hezekiah comes to power on the death of his father Ahaz, and calls on Egypt for aid against an ascendant Assyria. Isaiah points out the error of his ways. Then the land, together with the health of the king, is saved.

*Read Isaiah 39:1-8. Ah how tempting it is to be happy as long as our own life-times will be fine!*

Afterward, the pathway is cleared for exile and Babylon: Hezekiah displays God's Temple treasures to a Babylonian envoy. Oh foolish king! But he's okay. Nothing will go wrong until after he dies.

The next king, Manasseh, is renowned as evil, though he (maybe) repents (*2 Chronicles 33:10-13*). In Jewish tradition, he's the one who has Isaiah sawn in half. But a new prophet is rising…

Jeremiah begins his ministry in the time of King Josiah, grandson of Manasseh. Josiah is the good king, the great hope of the people. But Josiah dies young and things fall apart, yet again. Babylon conquers the world (or a large part of it), and the prophet survives repeated imprisonment and torture, only to see his land captured and his people scattered.

*Daniel 1:1-17 describes the first group taken into exile. Such captives would be groomed for positions of power and influence and were usually taken young—around age five or six.*

Among the first entering exile are the youthful elite of Jerusalem, including a boy called Daniel who refuses to eat the rich foods of his captors—refusing to betray the regulations of his home, and perhaps also protecting his digestion from the dangerously unfamiliar.

Daniel's story soon veers into the spectacularly supernatural. He interprets dreams (*Daniel 2*), just as Joseph did. He watches his friends walk around in a fiery furnace (*Daniel 3*). He allows himself to be called a magician (*Daniel 4:9*). He watches over a maddened king until his recovery (*Daniel 4:19-37*). He governs wisely into old age. And, many years after the time of King Nebuchadnezzar, he interprets the "writing on the wall" while decadent Babylon, under Belshazzar, falls prey to the Medo-Persians (*Daniel 5*). By then Daniel is an old man, but he continues in a position of power, opposed by the jealous, until his loyalty to God lands him in the lions' den (*Daniel 6*). God's favor continues to protect him all the way through to the reign of King Cyrus and the return from exile.

Meanwhile, Ezekiel is in the next group of exiles. These exiles are taken, not to work in court, but to work as laborers for their captors. They are housed far from Babylon itself, and Ezekiel becomes their prophet. His visions start with the amazing fiery chariot, wheels within wheels, faces within faces, and creatures within creatures (*Ezekiel 1*). Of course, fiery chariots weren't new: Elijah was taken up into heaven in one (*2 Kings 2:11*), and Elisha saw fiery chariots protecting the kingdom (*2 Kings 6:17*).

As captivity continues, Ezekiel becomes God's spokesperson to the exiles, and the go-to person for advice. He conveys information to a people who long to go home—who long for God to answer prayer and let them go. Through strangely silent pantomime and parables, he explains that Jerusalem will fall. Then his prophecy is fulfilled, and he speaks with words again.

Back in Jerusalem, Jeremiah speaks the same dire message (*Jeremiah 29:10-14*). And seventy years will pass before the exiles return—in the time of King Cyrus, as prophesied back in Isaiah (*Isaiah 44:28, 45:1,13*).

Some traditions hold that Cyrus released the exiles in awe at finding *his* name in *their* scriptures, making the fact that Isaiah knew his name important to the fulfilment of prophecy. But other traditions see Cyrus' policy as the next step in international politics, a deliberate contrast to Nebuchadnezzar's policy of transportation.

Some will claim that the works of Isaiah, which contained such appropriate messages for exile and return, might have been edited to include Cyrus' name as they were recited. Or, maybe, prophets from the *school* of Isaiah might have continued to preach and write in the style of Isaiah.

Should we argue over which tradition is right, with no way of knowing for sure until we die? Should we rejoice in Isaiah's knowledge of Cyrus' name, and complain that all others are wrong if they don't see things that way? Or should we accept that opinions differ, and delight in the sacred words?

Isaiah, Jeremiah, Ezekiel, Daniel and many other prophets of the time wrote many sacred words filled with meaning for the future and today. An exiled people, not surprisingly, had a serious interest in what the future would bring. Their longed-for return looms large. But equally looming is the message that this *return* won't be final; it won't heal all ills, and won't result in a people who unerringly follow God. That time is reserved for the future, for the promised "day of the Lord" and the ending of time...

...or perhaps for a closer future when the suffering servant of *Isaiah 53* will be seen—except that Jewish tradition maintains the servant is the city of Jerusalem—a city surely suffering to the present day. Could it be both?

Going back to the supernatural: Young Daniel, now grown old, has finally written down his visions, and readers still ponder what they might mean. But perhaps these visions need a chapter of their own.

Meanwhile, how do we, who read a Bible filled with supernatural voices, events, chariots and more, balance our faith in God's supernatural with the world's preoccupation with mystery and magic, or with our children's? I've heard people declare that fantasy's okay as long as it portrays a single all-powerful God. Fantasy board games *might* be okay if the priestly characters don't pray to foreign gods. Fantasy fiction mustn't include the recitation of spells. Magic must fail. God must be singular and good... We protect our families with well-wrought rules. And we turn those lovers of fantasy and fiction away from reading the Bible.

Do we really need to fence fantasy in with rules? Or should we instead concentrate, as Jesus told us, on watching for the "beam" in our own eyes rather than the "mote" in our neighbors' (*Matthew 7:5*). Perhaps the real *rule* is to keep *our* focus on God, the one true God, and pray (without judging) that our kids' focus will be held there too. Maybe pointing to God will help more than pointing out dangers in their literary, game-playing or movie-going pursuits. And maybe God will use fiction in mysterious ways to point to his truth. (Remember Balaam's donkey, the angel of death in Exodus, the accuser asking permission to wound Job's soul?)

Certainly God's prophets in the Bible sought to keep the focus where it belonged, from Isaiah (and before) foreseeing exile and healing, through Daniel balancing visions of kings and rulers with eternity, through to John, writing the book of Revelation after the suffering of Isaiah's Messiah, continuing that tale of the world's end to a place where modern analysts constantly miscalculate the dates… assuming, of course, the date can ever really be calculated (*Matthew 24:36*).

> *I've enjoyed learning more about prophets, prophecy, and the Biblically supernatural, by reading several Bible translations and commentaries side by side. Especially useful is the* Jewish Study Bible Tanakh Translation *from the Jewish Publication Society, Oxford University Press, ©1985, 1999 by the Jewish Publication Society.*

# Faith and Prophecy: After Daniel

The famous historian Josephus recounts how Alexander the Great, after crossing the Mediterranean Sea into the Western edge of Judea, set out to conquer the known universe. He arrived at the gates of Jerusalem where priests and leaders carried the book of Daniel to him. Over dinner (or over a feast), he was invited to see how the prophet Daniel, long dead by then, had foreseen the rise of Greece under its great leader. The Jewish God knew Alexander! *God* spoke about Alexander. *God* declared that Alexander would indeed be great. As a consequence, Alexander the Great continued his conquest of the known universe without attacking God's people.

They tell us we can test prophets by whether or not their words come true, but Daniel's distant visions didn't come true until long after his death. His even more distant, apocalyptic visions are yet to take place. Still, the people believed him a prophet and, if Josephus is to be trusted, they believed so firmly in him they shared his words with their enemies.

They trusted Daniel because his near-time prophecies did come true—he explained Nebuchadnezzar's dreams, foretold his madness, and predicted Belshazzar's fall; he saw the rise of a divided Medo-Persian empire; he saw the return of the Jews…

They trusted Daniel because of his faithfulness too—he wouldn't break faith with God's dietary rules; he wouldn't bow down to statues; he wouldn't stop praying… They trusted him because he was clearly touched by God—rising to power, but remaining faithful; never letting political expediency get in the way of prayer.

What prophets do we believe? Who do we trust, and why?

Should we believe the prophetic speaker on TV who declares that if so many dollars are raised, God will save the city? Should we believe the prophet in church who tells us we all need to march in a certain cause because God has called us to it? Should we believe that still small voice in the back of our mind that says take this job and God will shower blessings as reward?

Then, if we believe, how do we answer the grownup child or neighbor who declares we're just self-deceived? Can we really declare, if a promise comes true, that the prophecy must be from God? There's an oddly self-fulfilling touch to this. We can always be right, praising God for success and blaming those who didn't listen or obey whenever things go wrong. Meanwhile, our neighbor believes blessings come if we work hard enough; great causes are good on their own, without God's intervention; and the city will never be saved.

Of course, some will argue we *can't* trust Daniel either. Some claim he couldn't have predicted the things he did, and conclude parts of his book were written later, to give shape to history. Perhaps there's a self-fulfilling touch to this too—refuse to believe in prophecy, and therefore conclude a book of prophecy isn't what it claims to be. They might be right, of course. I'm no expert. But if they're right, then ancient Josephus, with no great axe to grind, is wrong. If they're right, new books (their late-written Daniel) were hidden among the old in the Dead Sea scrolls. And if they're right, we need some different explanation for why Alexander let Jerusalem stand.

I'd rather believe the simpler version of the story, that Daniel was a prophet, that his long-term prophesies were treasured by the Jews; protected and buried among the Dead Sea scrolls, not just because they were prophecy, but because they trusted in them. Daniel had survived lions, no less! So Daniel's word was good.

Which begs the question, how good is our word—in prophecy or in everyday life? How good is the word of people we call our prophets?

The next question of course is, did Daniel's prophecies really come true? Can we figure them out?

*Read Daniel 7:1-8 and remember Nebuchadnezzar's dream of the statue in Daniel 2:31-35.*

In Daniel's world, the great Nebuchadnezzar has died. His kingdom, symbolized by the golden head of the statue in his dream, is falling. Belshazzar probably rules in tandem with his father Nabonidus. There's profligate over-consumption at home, constant war abroad... And now Daniel sees what's to come.

The golden head of Nebuchadnezzar's statue matches the lion of Babylon in Daniel's vision. It's raised from the waters of chaos, but its wings have been plucked. Trials will come.

Nebuchadnessar's silver breastplate and shoulders are paralleled by Daniel's bear, raised up on one side. The Medo-Persians, who will soon conquer Babylon, represent a lopsided alliance between two nations. Called by God, they will "Arise" and "devour much flesh," or many kingdoms. But their reign won't last.

Next comes the four-winged leopard with four heads, paralleling those bronze thighs on Nebuchadnezzar's statue. If Greece is the leopard, the four heads represent the four divisions which will (and indeed did) arise after Alexander.

And then comes Rome—iron in Nebuchadnezzar's dream, and a dreadful, terrible, exceedingly strong monster in Daniel's. Rome is divided and falls into crumbling nations in Nebuchadnezzar's dream. Ten toes are made of clay and iron. Then a mighty rock destroys them.

*Read Daniel 7:13-14*

In Daniel's dream, Rome grows ten horns and another, boastful horn begins to destroy them. Then "one like the Son of man" is given dominion. Coming in the clouds of heaven before the Ancient of Days, he rules and all peoples serve him—hence "Son of Man" in the New Testament.

In some interpretations, Rome falls and ten kingdoms arise in Europe. Three are destroyed so completely they no longer exist. In other interpretations, ten is symbolic—the world will be split between random, countable numbers of kingdoms and empires. Others say there's a rule whereby prophets can't see the time between Christ's first and second coming; for them, Daniel's ten refers to ten kings who reappear in Revelation (*Revelation 17:12*). Not so long ago, Revelation's ten kings were *found* in the European Union... until its numbers increased to more than ten.

Daniel describes the fourth beast's reign as lasting a time, times and half a time (*Daniel 7:25*)—or maybe three and a half times... which is half of seven, which is a seriously symbolic number in the Bible. Six days of creation and on the seventh God rested—seven is the wholly perfect and perfectly whole completion of God's plan. So halfway through God's plan... halfway between creation and the end... is that when Jesus came?

Daniel's second dream takes place three years into Belshazzar's reign. While Daniel's still in Babylon, the vision transports him to Susa, which will soon become a major city of the Medo-Persian empire.

*Read Daniel 8:1-14*

Again an angel (remember Gabriel from the New Testament?) helps interpret the vision, though modern readers—their children and their neighbors—might wish God would send another angel to interpret his reply. A two-horned ram represents the two-sided kingdom of the Medes and the Persians. That's not too hard to imagine. Then the valiant goat which comes from the west (across the sea) must be Greece. And the ram has no power to stand up against the goat. No wonder Alexander the Great was pleased with this vision!

The male goat grows strong and its horn splits into four. Perhaps Alexander imagined four sons continuing his dynasty, but it wasn't to be. Instead, when Alexander died young, his kingdom became four separate entities—Lycandreans to the north (Lydia, Phrygia etc), Cassandreans to the west (Macedonia, Greece), Seluecids to the east (Iran, Iraq etc), and Ptolemies to the south (Egypt, Judea...). The Seleucids and the Ptolemies warred with each other, Judea becoming their battle-ground which switched from side to side. Meanwhile, Daniel sees one of the horns moving south (as the Seleucids would from Damascus), taking away the daily sacrifices in the Temple and trampling the sanctuary. With hindsight, this could well be the Seleucid ruler, Antiochus Epiphanes, as described in the book of Maccabees.

The sanctuary will be trampled for 2,300 days says the angel. Back in 1844, the Millerites interpreted those days as years and concluded the end of the world was at hand. They were wrong, as were those who thought the year 2,000 was the end. In practice, 2,300 could represent the days between the death of the High Priest and the death of Antiochus Epiphanes—the numbers fit, and that would certainly have encouraged readers at that time, just as Alexander was encouraged when he read about the ram.

But back to Daniel: As the time of return from exile approaches—seventy years, as predicted by Jeremiah—Daniel prays for the fulfilment of God's plan. Daniel's employed by the Medes now, restored to power after his foray into the lions' den. But the vision he receives is not of seventy years about to end, rather of seventy sevens of years just beginning. (Does this remind you of Jesus telling Peter how often to forgive—not seven times but seventy times seven *Matthew 18:22*?)

*Read Daniel 9:24-27*

Much effort has gone into interpreting the numbers in this prophetic vision. For example, seven weeks might be 7x7=49 years—the time taken to rebuild Jerusalem. 62 weeks could then be 434 years to the Messiah. But a *year* was only 360 days long, so 434 years takes us to 32AD, which might be the year Jesus died. And there's still one week left... perhaps that prophetically *invisible* time between the first and second coming?

If we analyze, dissect, and finally claim we know what this all means, we might end up like the Millerites, proven hopelessly wrong by events. On the other hand, if we claim we know nothing, how will we answer the question, why do we read?

Perhaps our best stance is to admit we don't know *everything*. In a world where Christians are renowned for sounding like they know best on every topic, that might be a seriously good stance!

Meanwhile, Daniel has one more vision for us. Cyrus has sent the first group of exiles home. Daniel is taking his prayer life very seriously with a three-week fast. And he sees one final vision.

*Do you see any similarities between Daniel 10:4-6 and Revelation 1:14-16?*

Daniel learns the names of angels, and the mysteries of angelic warfare

*Daniel 10:12-14 introduces Michael the archangel into the tale. Michael doesn't appear very often in the Bible. In Daniel 12:1-4 and Revelation 12:7-9 he's active at the end of time, and Jude retells a tradition that Michael helped bury Moses in Jude 9. Some people claim he's the archangel in 1*

*Thessalonians 4:16, and therefore that Jesus might be the human form of the archangel.*

Four more kings are prophesied to follow Cyrus—Cambyses, Pseudo-Smerdis, Darius Hystaspes, and Xerxes, who attacked Greece and failed miserably. Then Alexander the Great takes charge. As Daniel saw earlier, Alexander's kingdom splits into four. But this time there's more...

*Read Daniel 11:1-4*

The prophesy goes on to describe very accurately what happens to Judah under the divided kingdoms, with the Ptolemies to the south and Seluecids to the north. Berenice of Egypt marries Antiochus II (who first divorces a previous wife, Laodice). The alliance fails when the Ptolemaic leader dies, so Antiochus returns to his first wife who kills him, Berenice and their child. Ptolemy III takes offence, conquers the north and takes hostages...

*Read Daniel 11:5-8*

War continues. Antiochus III conquers lots of land before Egypt sends a huge army to defeat him. He turns east, amassing his own large armies from India. The Jews join forces with him in tackling Egypt again, imprisoning the Egyptian leader. Three armies fail to release him. But now Rome is rising so Antiochus cements a truce by marrying his daughter Cleopatra to Ptolemy V Epiphanes.

*Read Daniel 11:9-17*

Antiochus becomes overconfident, treats the Roman ambassadors badly, tries to conquer Greece and is defeated by the Roman, Scipio. His successor, now subject to Rome, imposes oppressive taxes and is poisoned, just after issuing an order to plunder the Temple. Then he's succeeded, somewhat deceptively, by Antiochus Epiphanes.

*Read Daniel 11:18-24*

The book of Maccabees tells the story. Antiochus suffers from broken treaties, takes out his frustrations on Judea, and has to surrender Egypt. Polluting the Temple altar with a pig and putting up an idol, probably to Zeus, he becomes the famous author of "the abomination of desolation" mentioned later in the New Testament.

*Read Daniel 11:25-35 and Matthew 24:15*

Thousands die. But what comes next?

By now, the skeptics claim with confidence that this book must have been written at a later date. Daniel can't have predicted all these events. Surely the story was written (albeit rather confusingly) with hindsight... but in that case:

- Why didn't Daniel name the kings (as Isaiah appeared to name Cyrus)?
- What about the non-Biblical story in Josephus, where Daniel's words caused Alexander the Great to move on?
- Why did the Jews preserve such supposedly *modern* writings so carefully among the Dead Sea Scrolls?

But this isn't the end of Daniel's vision. The story moves on with the promise of more to come. The antichrist arises. The end of it all is at hand. Or else, perhaps, this next vision is just further destruction wrought by Rome. But it is "at the time of the end," which often means the end of time... Revelation and apocalypse!

*Read Daniel 11:36-12:1*

Israel, either physically or metaphorically, is under attack. The archangel Michael (not Gabriel?) comes to her defense, and the book is sealed! So much for finding out those essential details about our future!

*Read Daniel 12:1-4. Lacking details here, try reading Zechariah 13:8, Deuteronomy 4:30, Jeremiah 30:7 as well.*

It's all going to last "a time, times and an half" again—three and a half times, or half of seven, again (*Daniel 12:7*). Or perhaps 1,290 days from the abomination of desolation... which is three and a half years plus 30, which is the age at which Jesus died... though 1,335 days takes us 45 years on, perhaps to the destruction of the Temple... Agh, so many numbers! And I a mathematician!

*Read Daniel 12:5-13*

There's lots of food for mathematics here; lots of food for possibly failed calculation; and lots of opportunity to remember, as Jesus reminded us, that nobody knows the date when the world will end.

So why does prophecy matter? Why do we read it? Why do we care? If someone accuses us of wanting to control the future, let's remind them, Daniel's knowledge didn't bring any immediate victories. All it brought was comfort to those living through dire times. Which is actually a pretty big thing.

God, who made us, who knows the future and the past, wants to bring us comfort in dire times—even such dire times as today!

God cares. God loves. And so should we.

> *To learn more about what happened to God's people from the time of Daniel to the present day, read* Letters to Auntie Fori *by Martin Gilbert.*

# Faith and Celebration: The Birth of Jesus

Christian faith is frequently seen as centering on the New Testament rather than Old. So maybe those three-and-a-halfs in Daniel really do mean Jesus came at the center point of time. Some might question if that center lies in Jesus' birth or in His death—counters of weeks have differing ideas—but what's 30 years in the lifetime of creation?

We certainly make a big display of celebrating Jesus' birth in the Christian world. Christmas brings its carols and songs, favorite readings and poems, cribs scenes and brightly lit trees. But Christmas under the shadow of crucifixion is a somewhat more complex concept. Easier, by far, just to rejoice in Santa Claus, based on the Christian Saint Nicholas' long-lost cause; let's enjoy a pine tree instead of a cross, adorned with pretty lights instead of blood. And then, let's complain that the world has secularized our favorite celebration! Our secular neighbors and subversive teens might justifiably remind us we secularized it all on our own. So what went wrong?

The Old Testament, as we know it, ends well before Alexander, Antiochus and Rome. But the books of Maccabees, while not generally accepted as divinely ordained, continue the history closer to the time of Christ. As do many other works…

Rebellion against Antiochus Epiphanes was followed by Judas Maccabees rededicating the ruined altar—around 164BC. Rome fought Carthage and conquered Corinth around 150BC. The Samaritan Temple is destroyed in 129BC. Galilee is conquered. Sadducees and Pharisees take opposing sides. And Israel is governed by a queen until the Sadducees seize back control. Jerusalem is under siege again, with a High Priest leading the attack in 65BC. Meanwhile, Pompey conquers the Syrians and Gaius Octavius, soon to be known at Augustus Caesar, is born around 63BC.

Julius Caesar defeats Pompey in 48BC, becoming ruler of Rome. Around the same time, Herod the Great becomes governor of

Galilee. Caesar is assassinated in 44BC, and Octavius, Mark Anthony and Marcus Lepidus rule Rome. Herod the Great becomes ruler of Judea as well as Galilee in 40BC, and becomes King in 37BC, a post he holds until his death in 4BC.

And, in the days of King Herod, an elderly priest, whose wife is too old to conceive, receives some very strange news. So does a girl, too young to be married. God, it seems, is no respecter of age.

It's hard for anyone to argue that Jesus (or John) didn't exist. Most people accept there was a man by his name (Jeshua—it's common enough) who lived his life and taught his words in his time in his place—in first-century Judea. Of course, there will always be those who disagree. But we can point to Josephus who mentions Jesus, and to others who mention the same names of rulers listed in the Gospels. Herod was king. Augustus was Caesar. Quirinius was governor of Syria. We even have records of a later census called by Augustus, even if this "first" one is only recorded in the Bible (as good a historical reference as any).

*Luke 2:1-5 specifies "first," which suggests Augustus ordered more than one census.*

The promised Messiah is born, according to Christian tradition, at just about the time predicted by Daniel. He sleeps in a manger—not so surprising or so uncomfortable—because there's no room at census time in the overcrowded town—likewise not so surprising. Imagine opening the door to your garage, leaving the car on the drive, and inviting distant relations to make use of the space. Isn't that what anyone would do? But... is this the story we advertise and celebrate?

Traditionally, *our* baby is wrapped in swaddling clothes in a dark, damp cave on the hillside. Some even suggest that such cloth, in such a cave, might be a shroud, which creates a beautifully symbolic image for us—life and death combined—but is it true? Maybe. Do we have to believe it to follow Christ? Probably not.

Rather like our dark, damp cave, the grave cloth / shroud is based on interpretation, not on words in the Bible. It's an intriguing idea, conveying a very cool message, but God's message matters more— that the child *was* born, in garage, cave or stable, and the Word was made flesh. That's what matters.

Tradition and interpretation affect other aspects of our celebration too. Those three kings crowding over the manger, their features representing those of the world's major nations perhaps—it's another cool message, but what does the Bible say?

*Matthew 2:1-12 includes some unexpected details, and excludes the familiar...*

Mary and Joseph might even have left their garage / stable and built their own small house now. Perhaps they'd set up a life for themselves in Joseph's ancestral town, and baby Jesus was a small child toddling around. The kings might have been wise men from Babylon (where the Israelites lived for so many years among people who followed stars)—though then why would the star be in the east since they'd surely travel west...? Ah, questions, questions...

Still, the wise men followed a star, and people are still trying to work out exactly what that star might have been. There was a supernova in around 5BC, which is probably when Jesus was born, but it was kind of small; while supernovas usually left large marks in human memories and historical records, this one is only recorded in one place. But supernovas don't move; how would it lead to Jerusalem then to Bethlehem, and how would it hover above a stable?

And if the star was a supernova, did it, as Arthur C. Clarke's science fiction short story "The Star" suggests, result in the destruction of a whole civilization—its planet lost in the sudden fire of its sun? Not a very pleasant thought.

There are lots of other intriguing interpretations of that star—even ones that get around those niggling questions. For a start, "star" might mean any heavenly body, and "in the east" might also be translated *at sunrise*. So my wise men, who I really want to hale from Babylon, could have followed a heavenly body that simply appeared at sunrise. Bethlehem's star could have been a comet, or a curious alignment of planets, the rising of Venus in a particular constellation... the possibilities are endless, and probably will never be narrowed down completely. After all, the only people who noted the event were astronomer kings who came to Bethlehem and left by a different path, so perhaps they rather deliberately didn't keep records.

Or the star could be a miracle, making the night truly as bright as day, as many believers say. My rational, teenage self had serious problems with that, as does my adult self. It's possible, but it's not essential—it's not the *only* interpretation that's faithful to the Bible. And we can still celebrate Christmas without a stellar miracle.

When the wise men fail to return to his palace, Herod sends his troops to Bethlehem to find the child. Tradition creates a scene of dire slaughter, small body parts flying through the air. But Bethlehem was a pretty tiny place. There probably weren't that many children under age two at the time, and, while we only know of one who escaped, there could well have been more.

The question I asked as a teen, though, was "Why age two?" But maybe the wise men came much later than the shepherds—maybe more than twelve days of Christmas later—and maybe Jesus really was a two-year-old toddler by then. And maybe the twelve days of Christmas come from some completely different kind of story.

Twelve is nicely symbolic of course—twelve tribes, twelve apostles, twelve months, four times three (which might be earth times God's unchangingness)... It's symbolic in other faiths too...

As is the winter solstice. But Christmas doesn't lie on the winter solstice. Christmas (December 25$^{th}$) doesn't coincide with pagan celebration (21$^{st}$), or even with Saturnalia, despite popular belief. It just happens to arise in the same month because...

Well, Christmas takes place, intriguingly, nine lunar months after Easter (at least, as it was understood in around 200AD). And nine months is the time from conception to birth. Thus Christ's human life is conceived (symbolically speaking) on the same calendar day as his death—a date that, unfortunately, was calculated using two different calendars in the East and West, giving two different dates—December 25$^{th}$ and January 6$^{th}$. When East and West met, rather than argue the date of Jesus' birth, the churches accepted both dates, with twelve days of Christmas between them.

Of course, we know more about that calendar now than our predecessors did. Hence, with historical evidence for Herod's death in 4BC, we suggest that Christ was born around 6 or 5BC. Numerically illogical, but still... we always knew our interpretations were humanly flawed.

So now we Christians have BC, for before Christ, and AD for Anno Domini (year of our Lord), while the secular world has BCE and CE (the common era). Meanwhile Jews and others count years in their own different ways, and we never quite learn to humanly agree. Can we disagree in love? Can we share our mixed up celebrations with love? Can we delight that others celebrate Hannukah, Kwanzaa, or simply Santa Claus at the same time as Christmas? Or must we always complain they're not celebrating the *right* thing in the *right* way (with the *right* number of wise men as well)?

Is delight or complaint more likely to lead others to look at or share in our faith?

The Bible includes lots of stories of celebration. It doesn't tell us when Christians started celebrating Jesus' birth. It doesn't give us a date for when he was born. But it does bring us joy.

> *For more information on the origins of Christmas and the way we celebrate, read* All Things Christmas *by E. G. Lewis.*

# Faith and Hope: The Story of Jesus

There seems little doubt that a historical Jesus lived in the region of Judea around the year 30AD. His followers, starting from an insignificant corner of the Roman Empire, somehow changed the world, so much so that even Josephus complains about the man they believe rose from the dead. And Christians today, just like those early Christians, really believe Jesus rose from the dead. We really believe that Jesus does change the world, each and every day. And we believe we have a God who, in Jesus, knows exactly how it feels to be human!

If my grown up child says, "He was just a man," I'll ask him how such an unimportant man caused so much change. If he says, "It was just that his disciples were great speakers, and the timing was right, and it's all coincidence," I'll remember that God manufactures the best coincidences. And I'll go back, always, to that question of "Who moved the Stone?" (a book by Frank Morison). Because great speakers, good timing, and convenient coincidences don't empty graves—and Jesus rose!

Still, that stone wasn't moved until after Jesus' death. First came real life, real ministry, real humanity, and real hope for people who really did live (rather hopelessly) in an insignificant corner of the Roman Empire. Real hope for us too, if we believe God knows what human hopelessness feels like!

At that (real, historical) time of Jesus' birth, Israel, under Rome, was ruled by Herod the Great, not the kindest, greatest or most Jewish of men. Jesus' parents were both of priestly families (according to Matthew's and Luke's genealogies), and had probably fled from Judea to Galilee to avoid the various conscriptions Herod undertook to build his fortresses. The birth of a savior to parents fleeing unfair government surely offers *hope for those traveling in search of better lives.*

Jesus' parents weren't even married at the time of his conception. Neighbors could have turned them out of church, but luckily didn't. *Hope for those who don't fit in with society's rules?*

With Mary heavily pregnant, Joseph took his family back to the family home in Bethlehem to file for Roman taxation. The streets and houses were filled with returnees, and there was scarcely room for traditional hospitality. Still, the baby was born in a manger. *Hope for the poor, the overcrowded, those helpless in the face of government regulation...*

But Herod heard a rumor that this child might be a king and sent soldiers to kill him. Joseph had probably established a carpentry business by now in Bethlehem. But he couldn't stay. So Joseph and Mary fled to Egypt, probably to one of those small Jewish villages established long ago along the border. Luckily, the Egyptians didn't kick them out. *Hope for refugees.*

On the death of Herod, waiting till Jesus is maybe four or five years old, the family returns. But Bethlehem still isn't safe for them. Herod's son, Herod Archelaus, is a cruel ruler, and they flee back to Nazareth. *Hope for those who've given up and gone home.*

Jewish tradition required those, who could travel, to visit Jerusalem for the Festivals each year. But Jesus doesn't go to Jerusalem until he's twelve years old—until that second Herod has been replaced by the Romans. Now the carpenter's son visits his heavenly father in the Temple and is famously lost (and found). *Hope for the lost and those who've lost them. Hope for those unable to follow tradition. Hope for those who feel left out.*

After this, the gospel stories gloss over Jesus' childhood. The young man (at twelve he was almost adult) becomes a carpenter, lives with his earthly parents, and does nothing to stir the pot of history. *Hope for the quiet, the unknown, those without influence.*

But, as age thirty approaches, a visit to Jerusalem changes everything. Jesus is baptized by his cousin John and hears the voice of God. According to the gospels, others also hear the voice, but not everyone. Then Jesus retires to the desert to prepare for ministry. *Hope for those who hear, who maybe hear, who can't quite tell what they've heard, who need to go to a quiet place and pray... and for those who are tempted, as Jesus faces and conquers temptation with words from the Bible.*

On his return, Jesus starts picking up disciples—Andrew and John from the crowd around John the Baptist, Simon brother of Andrew, and then Philip, probably another fisherman visiting Jerusalem, and then Nathaniel. *Hope for those whose jobs seem unimportant, for those who read too much (like Nathaniel), and for those who've wandered away and need to come back (like Simon, brought back by his brother).*

Still teaching and preaching near Jerusalem, they set up a baptismal ministry rivaling that of John the Baptist, and attract the attention of the rich and influential Nicodemus. *Hope for the influential too!*

But John the Baptist is arrested for preaching against Herod Antipas' marital machinations. Since Jesus' "time has not yet come" (a phrase he will soon use in Cana as his public ministry begins, and again in Jerusalem shortly before the end), he heads north, back to Nazareth and beyond in Galilee. En route he passes through Samaria and talks with the most un-influential of all people—a Samaritan woman. *Hope for rejects, outcasts, and for women!*

A short stay in Nazareth leads to the team being invited to a wedding where the wine runs out. Mary asks Jesus for help and he tells her his time has "not yet come," but helps all the same. *Hope for those who feel like their prayers aren't being answered... yet.*

Jesus speaks in his local synagogue, but Nazareth doesn't welcome him—isn't he just the carpenter's son? So he sets off with his friends for Capernaum by the Sea of Galilee. *Hope for nobodies and carpenter's sons I guess, and for rejects too.*

Galilee is where those fishermen followers grew up. It's where Simon lives with his wife and mother-in-law. It's where James and John run their father, Zebedee's, boat, where Matthew will soon be seen collecting taxes, and where other new disciples—Judas Iscariot who may well be a "spy" for the Jerusalem authorities, Simon the Zealot who probably has ties to rebels in the mountains, James son of Alphaeus (who may be Matthew's brother), Judas Thaddeus (who may be another brother or cousin), and Thomas the Twin whose eponymous "twin" could even be a female follower. All are welcomed as Jesus' followers. *Hope for all of us too!*

Simon's mother-in-law is healed and serves dinner. Meanwhile Jesus' fame spreads through the region and crowds start to gather. It's time to slip back out into the countryside, where Jesus heals a leper! *Hope for the sick, and for those who feel completely cast out by society.*

Returning to town, Jesus heals a man who's let down through the roof, because the streets are too crowded for friends to get him to the door. *Hope that where there's a will, there really might be a way.*

But Jesus doesn't just heal the paralyzed man—he heals his sins as well. *Hope for sinners.*

And he heals on the Sabbath! *Hope for those who might not interpret God's rules quite the same way as we do.*

Then the crowds follow Jesus out of town. He prays on a mountaintop and preaches to the assembled populace. It's a pretty famous sermon, and it's full of messages that turn the world upside down. *Hope for the poor in spirit. Hope for those who mourn. Hope for the meek and the quiet. Hope for those who hunger for God to fix things. Hope for the merciful (and for those needing mercy perhaps). Hope for the pure in heart (who may actually be different from those who* purely *follow what they think are God's laws, as the Pharisees do). Hope for peacemakers (even if peace seems unachievable). Hope for those who are persecuted (but does that include those who only think they're being persecuted?). Hope!*

Maybe it's one sermon. Maybe it's many combined into one. Jesus probably repeated the same points to different crowds in different places. But readers of the gospel will hear them repeated today, and we just might have to learn to love our enemies (*Luke 6:17-36*). We may need to be wary of anger and judgement in our relationships (*Matthew 5:21-26, 7:1-5*). And we might have to pray with forgiveness in our hearts (*Matthew 6:9-13, Luke 11:1-4*).

Jesus heals a centurion's servant without even seeing him. *Hope for those who feel far from God, and for those who pray for them.*

He heals in crowds and in private. He travels with the support and help of women! He heals both physical and demonic illnesses. *Hope for those who don't even know what they need healing from.*

He meets the rich and the poor and shares meals (and discussions) with them, even if they happen to be despised tax-collectors. *Hope for the despised.*

He refuses to go home when his family chase after him. *Hope for those who are lacking in family support.*

He refuses to give up when people accuse him of working with Satan. *Hope for those lacking church support too, as long as they, like Jesus, are truly steeped in prayer.*

And he tells stories. *Hope for storytellers like me!*

One day he walks on water toward his disciples. Perhaps it's a reminder of God parting the Red Sea. Simon leaps out to join him, takes a few steps and sinks, but Jesus saves him. *Hope for us when our faith just can't keep up.*

Traditionally, Jesus' ministry lasts three years, which really isn't long. *Hope for those who are waiting to start, and for those too soon finished.*

He travels beyond the boundaries of Israel, teaching and healing, and arguing, even with pagans. *Hope for those who don't belong.*

And he retains a sense of humor—try reading a more modern translation to hear those crazy undertones: when a woman argues that even the dogs eat crumbs from under the table; when hyperbole tells you to cut out your own eye so you won't be tempted; when a healed man is told to "stop sinning or something worse may happen to you." *Hope for those who take everything seriously, and for those who don't.*

But his time has not yet come. Even in his final year, Jesus avoids the first crowds of the Feast of Tabernacles, arriving at the Temple quietly, halfway through the week. There he tells people he'll soon be gone, and they think he might be heading for pagan lands or even planning to kill himself! (*John 7:35-36, 8:21-22*). *Hope for those who take forever to understand perhaps.*

Then it's back to Galilee, until that final journey begins, for a final Passover. Poor Thomas, well-remembered now as the doubter, is the one who declares, "Let's go and die with him." (*John 11:16*) So there's *hope for the hopeless, and for doubters too!*

On that final journey, Jesus and his disciples all crowd into the home of Jesus' dear friends Martha, Mary and Lazarus. But not until poor Lazarus is dead! *Hope for the dead? Hope, at least, for the bereaved.*

And now we enter a final week, where Jesus is hailed by the crowds on entering Jerusalem, through the very same gate through which the glory of God departed long ago in *Ezekiel 10*. *Hope for those who love looking for Biblical symbols and parallels!*

More Temple arguments ensue, including a famous scene where Jesus throws out the moneychangers. *Hope for those who wish things were different.*

Mountainside discussions cover the end of Jerusalem and the end of the world. A fig tree withers. Judas complains that money spent on ointment could have been used to feed the poor, and Jesus tells us the poor will always be among us. *Hope, I guess, for those who fear neither good politics nor good policies will change the world, but a better end is coming.*

And then we find one final meal, secretly prepared and shared. With no servants handy, Jesus washes his own disciples' feet. *Hope for us, when we feel we're asked to do something we'd rather not undertake.*

He sends the one who will betray him on his way. *Hope for us when we see things fall apart. God has a plan.*

He goes out to pray and asks if it has to be this way. *Hope for us when if-onlys wear us down. God has a plan.*

He's arrested, and fighting doesn't help. *God has a plan.* He's taken before the authorities and honesty doesn't help. He's charged, and Pilate's reluctance to convict him doesn't help. He's scourged and the offer of an honest way out doesn't help. And he's taken out to die. *But God has a plan!*

Three days later Jesus rises from the grave... Or three nights, or three somethings—from Friday afternoon to night, one day; from Friday night to Saturday night, a second day; from Saturday night to an empty tomb at dawn on the third day. And the resurrection is a message of *hope to all*! Death is conquered. Injustice is conquered. Unbelief, cruelty, despair... all our human trials are conquered because the divine has entered and shared them all, and is alive!

So that's what we know about the historical Jesus, the "man" who also claimed to be "the son of Man," who said "I am" when those words were outright heresy (unless he was God), who performed and promised miracles (how cruel if he couldn't perform them), who forgave sins (which no man could do)... And who, if he wasn't God, was surely (as C. S. Lewis suggested) either mad or bad.

Which leaves us still with the question of who moved the stone. Nobody went to worship at Jesus' tomb, because no body was there. Nobody denied that the body was gone. The priests, the soldiers, the church and civil authorities, anyone who could have disproved the resurrection surely would have—after all, this insignificant blot on the Roman Empire mustn't be allowed to get ideas beyond itself. Besides, the Pax Romana, bought at such a high price, required that rules and regulations be obeyed; and dead rebels don't rise.

When the grown-up rebel child declares that those unkempt fishermen were *just such great speakers*, that the Biblical parallels are *just coincidence*, that the miracles were *just good luck* and the teaching *just good wisdom*, and that Jesus was nothing more than a man, I'll continue to answer, "Who moved the stone?" And I'll continue to live with faith and hope for the future.

> *For more about that stone, read Frank Morison's* Who Moved the Stone *or J.N.D. Anderson's* Evidence for the Resurrection, *or any of the many more modern books on the subject.*
>
> *For more about whether Jesus was mad, bad or God, read* Mere Christianity *by C. S. Lewis.*
>
> *And to read how interpretation has blurred that hope-filled message through history, read* Correcting Jesus *by Brian Griffith*

# Faith and Love: The Story of Salvation

So the story comes full circle. One simple rule was quickly broken in the Garden of Eden. Ten Commandments couldn't save God's chosen people. 623 laws couldn't make us fit to enter God's presence. Then Jesus offered two laws and refined them to one new law, one new commandment even... and saved us with love.

The Old Testament is filled with examples of those who knew God's law, behaving as if they didn't—rich kings demanding excessive taxes, threatened rulers making unholy alliances, contented people forgetting the God who saved them... Even the New Testament's new church reveals a people divided: law-keepers, law-breakers, law-changers... endless arguments over meeting and eating with Gentiles... do Christians have to first become Jews... is non-kosher meat-eating allowed...?

But in Jesus, God has (and surely always had) a better way. Knowing we really can't obey, He truly does save us with love! And we can't obey. No matter how good we think we are, no matter how many commandments we think we've never broken, we are all sinners; we all need to be saved; and we can *only* be saved with love—likewise our children and our neighbors! And God just might surprise us by who He lets into heaven.

*Matthew 7:3-5 reminds us we all have sin in our lives, and however large we may think our neighbor's sin (or our child's, or our child's best friend's), it's a speck compared to the plank (a mote compared to the beam) that's clouding our vision.*

Jesus' ministry emphasized love. He even gave a new commandment (though some interpret it to only apply to *the saved*).

*Read John 13:34-35. What do you think? Should we only love church members? If so, what about Mark 12:30-31?*

But non-Christians don't always see us as loving, or loveable. Is that their fault, God's fault, or ours?

Non-Christians (and teenage children of Christians) don't always see how a loving God might want His son to die on a cross either. Or how a loving God would allow His world to get into the mess it's in; war, famine, plague, global warming... couldn't God fix these if He really loved us? Couldn't God keep children from dying before their time, keep parents from losing their jobs, keep those in pain safe from addiction?

Replying that it's a broken world is a bit too easy. Explaining things away with "Well, He suffered the death of His son" still leaves people asking why. We might be better off just saying we don't understand; we don't understand, but we know God loves us. And then we look again at God's story of love.

God loved Adam and Eve and gave them just one rule for keeping their perfect world—the perfect Garden of Eden—perfect forever. And they broke it, because that's what we do. Then God loved His people and gave them 10 rules, plus 613 guidelines to interpret those rules. And they broke them. Then God loved us still and gave two rules—"Love God, and love your neighbor as yourself." But even these defeat us, even now when we've experienced the mess that disobedience creates. Unfortunately, perfect worlds and messes don't mix. So God sent Jesus to pay for and clean up our mess (*John 3:16*), so we could still belong in His perfect presence.

God loved His people and chose one nation as the nursery, or family, through which we could be saved. He chose Abraham and modeled love by asking for, then sparing the life of Abraham's son (*Genesis 22:13*). It seems a strange model of love to us, but it made cultural sense at the time, and it instituted the truth that substitutions can be made, that someone or something else can pay for us.

God rescued His people from Egypt, instituting sacrifice for sin, sacrifice for the journey, and sacrifice for commitment. Then He rescued His people from sin with one perfect sacrifice. Does that mean death is a punishment for sin? Or does it just mean death is a consequence of sin (as Genesis suggests)? Or... can we just say, we don't know?

The parallels are interesting though:

- *Luke 19:38, Exodus 12:1-6.* The lamb is chosen four days before it's eaten, and Jesus was hailed (or chosen) as Messiah ("Blessed

be the King that cometh in the name of the Lord") four days before his crucifixion.
- *Matthew 22:15-40, Exodus 12:5.* The lamb is examined to confirm its perfection, and Jesus was examined by the authorities. Of course, they didn't find him perfect, but God did at the Transfiguration (*Matthew 17:2-5*)
- *John 12:1-8.* Jesus is anointed, as is the sacrificial lamb.
- *Mark 11:15, Exodus 12:8.* Leaven is removed from the house at Passover, and the moneychangers were removed from the Temple.
- *Read Mark 15:34* Jesus died at the ninth hour (3 o'clock), when the lambs were being sacrificed in the Temple.

A sacrifice long ordained perhaps? Meanwhile, Jesus prayed forgiveness for those who crucified him—now that's love! And God, accepting that final sacrifice, showed His acceptance by raising Jesus from the dead.

After the resurrection, Jesus' disciples began to teach and preach in his name. John wrote:

- *John 3:16*—"God so loved the world"
- *John 13:34-35*—"A new commandment"
- *John 15:13*—"Greater love hath no man"
- *1 John 3:1*—"Behold what manner of love"
- *1 John 4:7-10*—"Beloved, let us love one another"
- *1 John 4:19-21*—"We love him, because he first loved us"
- *1 John 5:3*—"For this is the love of God"
- *2 John 1:6*—"And this is love"

Meanwhile Paul, not renowned for being lovable, wrote:

- *Romans 5:8*—"God commendeth his love toward us"
- *Romans 12:10*—"Be kindly affectioned… with brotherly love"
- *Romans 13:10*—"Love worketh no ill"
- *1 Corinthians 13:1*—"Though I speak… and have not charity"
- *1 Corinthians 13:13*—"… the greatest of these is charity"
- *Galatians 5:14*—"Thou shalt love thy neighbor as yourself"
- *Galatians 5:22*—"But the fruit of the Spirit is love"
- *Ephesians 2:4*—"But God… for his great love"

- *Ephesians 3:19*—"...love of Christ, which passeth knowledge"
- *Ephesians 4:2*—"... forbearing one another in love"
- *Ephesians 5:2*—"... as Christ also hath loved us"
- *Philippians 2:2*—"... having the same love"
- *Colossians 3:14*—"And above all these things put on charity"
- *1 Thessalonians 3:12*—"... increase and abound in love"
- *1 Thessalonians 4:9*—"... taught of God to love one another"

A faith filled with love, indeed (sometimes translated as charity). If only we could display the love we preach.

But what about those *big* questions that Christians are so renowned for pronouncing on? What about abortion, euthanasia, the death penalty, divorce, a woman's place in the home, homosexuality, transgender rights, slavery even...? If we want to speak condemnation to these, we might have to be sure we don't ourselves stand condemned by God's own voice in the New and Old Testament.

> *Isaiah 58:6-7 is just one of many passages reminding us to care for the poor and the hungry. Amos 4 condemns idolatry and its consequences. The rich get richer...*
>
> *And Jesus reminds us that what we do to others might just as well be done to Him in Matthew 7:21-23.*

That doesn't mean we shouldn't have opinions, or even voice opinions on right and wrong. But perhaps it means we should voice those opinions caringly, and we should be aware that others, who also love God, might not share our interpretation of God's law. And that those who interpret His law differently are neither greater nor lesser sinners than we, neither in greater nor lesser need of forgiveness and God's love. For example:

- In early Christian days, the question of *when* a soul entered a body was still debatable. Can we really claim to have finally solved it today?
- In early Christian days, the desperately ill could not be kept alive by medicine, or forced to take nourishment. Can we really claim we know exactly how much medicine and nourishment God will allow, and what treatment is forbidden?

- In early Christian days, sexuality was deeply tied to pagan religious practice. Do we know for sure that the passages we quote referred to private sexuality as well as public?

We may know. We may be completely sure. But that doesn't give us the right to condemn our neighbor who *knows* otherwise, nor to call him or her or them a fool… because, didn't Jesus say something about calling people fools being the same as murder?

And didn't Jesus die to save us… by love, not law?

> *I learned a lot about the connection between the Passion and Passover from reading* In Three Days *by E. G. Lewis*

# Faith and Words: The Story of the Church

Sadly, love probably isn't the first thing people think of as characterizing Christianity. We may have done much that's good in the world, but Christians (in name anyway) also brought the Inquisition, torture, forced conversions and more. Christians (in name) brought terror to the streets of Northern Ireland. And Christians (in name) still turn certain sinners away from their churches' doors. So what went wrong?

The verses, describing love, in the last chapter probably sound about the same, whichever Bible translation you use to look them up. But not all verses sound the same in different Bibles, and not all translations (and interpretations) are the same as each other. Have you ever wondered where those "some translations don't include this passage" comments come from in your Bible? Or "other translations say..." Are we allowed to wonder about this, or does choosing any version other than the KJV make us lesser Christians? Does wanting to know what *the original* said make us doubters? And when we, or our children, learn we can't actually know what the originals said, because they were lost long centuries ago, what will we do now?

The Christian faith spread out from Jerusalem after Jesus' resurrection and ascension into heaven. Paul tried to stamp out this heresy, then found himself in the forefront of the converted. Missionaries traveled across land and sea, to Turkey, Greece, Italy, even Spain. Mark wrote his *short* account of what Jesus said and did. Matthew, the Jewish scholar, and Luke, the intellectual Gentile, wrote their own versions, based on Mark's writing and other, long-lost documents or private conversations. Later, John wrote a smoothly literary, well-wrought gospel. Meanwhile, Paul was writing letters to people and churches from his travels. Peter, James, Jude... more letters ensued. And we have no access to any originals of any of these—not a single one!

What we do have access to are copies, fragments, references ("As Paul said in his letter to..." etc.), then later copies, then more until whole books were put together, until rival collections of authorized scriptures were molded (with much prayer and long discussion) into one.

Some argue that the dates I've suggested are all wrong; that everything was written much, much later by different people. Certainly the copies and fragments we have, from much later, were transcribed by different people. And those fragments don't always agree, word for word, with each other, never mind with the unfound *original*. But what does that prove?

Did John really write the first chapter of his gospel, even though the language is more cultured and lyrical, or was it added afterward—or did John himself add it afterward as he grew more educated about his work?

Did Jesus really forgive the woman caught in adultery, and did John or Luke write about it? The chapter is found in Luke as well as John, and in different parts of John from where we see it today.

Did Jesus ever refer to himself as God or the Son of God?

Much though we'd like to believe those early Christians were united, clearly they weren't. Even in Acts, church leaders argued vehemently over circumcision, eating with Gentiles, what meat should be allowed on the Christian table... As the church expanded, the problems only got worse. Could those who said Jesus was just a man be included among Christians? If not, what should Gospel transcribers do about passages referring to Jesus' mother and father (*Luke 2:41-52 in some versions*)? Maybe change the word to parents? And those who said Jesus was God, and not man at all—could God sweat blood (*Luke 22:44*)? Maybe the scribes should keep in or take out that passage.

Ancient records, fragments of records, and references to records, frequently include the same words with slight textual changes, and textual analysts are left trying to guess which version was original. Add in those innocent errors of transcription—accidents from trying to copy while tired perhaps, and there are errors upon errors...

Some argue there are so many errors it's pointless to believe in anything. Others—perhaps those with a more mathematical bent—instead express surprise that there aren't more errors. Whatever the disagreements, however we interpret what we *think* was original, the fact is the story survived—an amazing, well-documented story of a real historical character who shouldn't, by any stretch of human imagination, have had such a huge impact on the world.

Perhaps the important question is not which version (which words) do you believe, but how do you believe—with love for those who might not agree with you, or with Inquisition-style opposition? What would Jesus do?

Initially, Christian Jews probably lived near the River Jordan (for baptisms) outside Jerusalem. They held all things in common (*Acts 2:44*) like Communists, or at least socialists; and attended synagogue on Saturdays because they were Jews. Perhaps they celebrated Communion on Sundays, or perhaps that came later. (Some say the choice of Sunday as the Christian Sabbath had as much to do with Jewish rules about not walking on a Saturday as with the day of Jesus' resurrection.) But the efforts of these early Messianics to convert their neighbors got Stephen killed, and the camp-dwellers scattered.

Paul the Pharisee felt a sacred calling to round up and punish the rebels, but found himself converted outside Damascus. After this he either returned to Jerusalem or wandered alone in the desert to study God's word. Either way, his efforts to convert the population of Damascus were doomed to failure—who wants to be converted by someone who's going to put you in jail? So he ended up in Jerusalem, defending himself before Christians he'd once persecuted. Moving on seemed a wise move, so Paul traveled with Barnabas, eventually landing in Antioch and working with the Christian church there.

When famine struck (as documented in other books besides the Bible), Paul joined a team bringing food to the downtrodden Christians of Jerusalem. Much discussion on the conversion of Gentiles ensued. Christians seemed moderately united at this point, but a split soon arose causing a rift between Peter and Paul. The rift wouldn't be healed for several years. Meanwhile, Paul traveled around Galatia and Peter headed for Rome.

Jews and Christians in Rome began to argue and riot over the identity of the Messiah. Soon both groups were thrown out of town. So Paul, Peter and others headed to Jerusalem for further Jew-Gentile negotiations. The decision was made that Christians only needed to avoid meat with blood in it, things offered to idols (which included lots of meats), and *fornication* (which could mean sexual behavior offered to idols, depending on your interpretation).

Paul set off on another journey, carrying Christianity to Troy and from there to the Greek peninsula and Athens. Afterward he returned to Jerusalem then Antioch, rested a while, and set off on his "third missionary journey." He wanted to go to Rome on the way to Spain, but his travel plans were thwarted by famine and persecution.

Back in Jerusalem Paul was arrested and imprisoned. Luke might have hung around with him, writing Acts, while Paul wrote various letters. Eventually a new governor was appointed and needed to sort out the prison population. Paul appealed to Rome, so he got there in the end, via shipwreck, snakebite and more! (Who says the Bible's boring? *Oh yeah, that was me!*)

Some believe Paul died in Rome during this imprisonment. Others say he was released and maybe even made it to Spain. Luke wasn't there though, so he didn't write about it—instead we're left to guess what Paul did from his letters and other sources. And guesswork, not surprisingly, leaves space for disagreement. Whatever the timing though, most people agree Paul was finally killed in Rome, and that Peter, also killed in Rome, was Bishop of Rome at some point—hence the first *Pope*.

Meanwhile Emperor Nero, who'd been busy killing people and persuading people to commit suicide, committed suicide himself. Ignatius, a friend of Peter and Paul, became Bishop of Antioch, and Linus (another friend) became Bishop of Rome.

Rebels in Jerusalem continued to cause problems for Rome, and around 70AD the Temple was destroyed, ending centuries of Jewish sacrifices. Masada fell soon afterward. Vesuvius erupted, burying Pompeii. Cletus became the next bishop of Rome. The Coliseum (still around today!) was dedicated! And in 90AD, the Jewish council at Jamnia met to discuss which Jewish texts would be accepted as scriptural (the first of many such meetings).

John was exiled to Patmos (or imprisoned—again, depending on your interpretation) and wrote Revelation. (Of course, in some interpretations, this is a different John from John the disciple.) Pope Clement followed Pope Cletus and was followed by Pope Evaristus—the first to set priests over parishes! Then Pope Alexander, in 107AD, was first to bless homes with "holy water." Meanwhile, Trajan and Pliny wondered what to do about Christians in Bythinia—a troublesome lot we are!

Sixtus became Pope, or Bishop of Rome, in 115AD, and Hadrian (who built that wall and those long straight Roman roads in Britain) became emperor in 117AD. And so on.

Some of these things are accepted as known and incontrovertible. Others remain debatable. It all depends how much corroborating evidence is found—in archeology, in unrelated writing, in textual analysis… Because history is inherently long and complicated, and hard to *experiment* on.

Working out what happened when, why and how—analyzing the words of the Word—is a task best left to the experts (and I'm not one). Fitting the Bible and Bible people into the story is, again, a task for those who know much more than I. But it's a fascinating task, and it's intriguing to learn how our different denominations and disagreements are indeed "no new thing under the sun" (*Ecclesiastes 1:9*).

> *A great place to learn about errors and changes in New Testament translations is the book,* Misquoting Jesus *by Bart D. Ehrman. The author may be agnostic now, but his arguments and investigations shouldn't in any way detract from the reader's faith.*

# Faith and Symbols: Revelation

So we reach the final book in our Christian Bible, written from the Island of Patmos by a man named John. But who is John? Why is he on Patmos? And more importantly, why is he writing such a very strange book?

Not surprisingly, no one knows for sure when or by whom Revelation was written. Tradition suggests the author is John the Apostle, writing before the fall of the Temple in Jerusalem—after all, the book never references the Temple's destruction, which must surely have been a huge event; and it does say "John" wrote it. And a God-wins-in-the-end book would be a logical thing to write as such an awful time approached. But there are equally valid arguments for a later date, at which point John becomes someone else entirely (or else an extremely long-lived individual). Will arguing one way or the other advance anyone's faith?

Most people either love or hate the book of Revelation. Personally, I love it. As a child I loved the amazing imagery. It didn't upset me that locusts looked like horses with lions' teeth, ladies' hair, and scorpions' tails (*Revelation 9:7-10*)—I viewed it all as something beyond the ability of words to describe. And, as a lover of words, that thought awed and astounded me.

Now, as an adult, I love Revelation even more for the symbolism behind its events and imagery. But again, symbols can always be interpreted differently. I like my approach—I borrowed most of it (with permission) from Dr. Jon Garvey—but I'm not going to argue that it's better than anyone else's. The truth, as ever and always, is more than I know. But I'll offer it here in case it inspires you to love a book you've once hated, or to answer those questions your neighbors might throw at you (like locusts can't have lions' teeth, ladies' hair, and scorpions' tails so how can you believe anything that the Bible says?).

**First, there's THE AUTHOR.**

John is exiled to Patmos. He appears to have some authority over seven churches, to whom he sends letters. So he's probably a bishop. And he's probably been sent to Patmos to stop him from turning seven churches into seventy. But is he John the apostle, another John who followed Jesus, or even a much later John? Christians have argued this since the 4<sup>th</sup> century. But I'll go with John the Apostle, for simplicity.

In which case, who exiled John, and when? The emperor Domitian reigned in Rome from 81-96 AD and was known for exiling, rather than killing, opponents. If he exiled John, then the exile occurred after the destruction of the Temple (in 70 AD). But John may have been exiled by a governor rather than an emperor—perhaps the governor of Asia, in which case exile *to* Patmos means exile *from* the mainland. Again, no one knows for sure, but I'll go with the earlier date.

And then, where was John? In jail? There's a cave on Patmos that's advertised as his cell. Or in a house, because the only rule was he mustn't convert people and he mustn't return? I like the idea of a house because it helps me write *Five-Minute Bible stories* about children who met him—how's that for a totally irrelevant reason?

But most importantly...

**WHAT SORT OF BOOK did John write?**

Revelation is also called "The Apocalypse," and apocalypses were really not uncommon in prophetic writings. Daniel wrote one. Ezekiel wrote one. And now John wrote as well. Like Ezekiel, his book is set around a vision of heaven, represented by God's Temple. But in John's book, the writer doesn't measure the Temple; instead he's invited inside to the worship service. And we get to join him!

Apocalypses were often written when things were going wrong in the world; at times when hearts and minds might rightly be concerned with God's overall plan. An apocalypse offers the assurance that's God's in control, the comfort of knowing there really will be an end to all our trials, and a vision, perhaps, for the immediate future that offers immediate hope.

Another thing apocalypses have in common is symbols: numerical symbols such as 2 for trust, 3 for certainty, 4 for the earth's four corners and winds, 6 for trust in God (2x3) or for wrongness and falling short (falling short of 7 perhaps), 7 for God's right plan (on the seventh day God rested), 10 for the humanly countable (like fingers on our hands), 12 for God's choice (disciples and tribes), and 40 for a long time. There are cultural symbols too—

precious stones, lampstands, double-edged swords... And then there's the form of symbolic imagery that *reads* through pictures. Imagine how someone who's never seen a cartoon strip would interpret a star-shape with *BAM* written inside it; perhaps we can't imagine those strange locusts because we haven't learn how to read the right cartoons.

## So WHERE DO WE BEGIN?

John's vision starts with a wealth of Old Testament references—the faithful witness, first born of the dead, coming on clouds, deserving glory and dominion. It's a vision of Jesus, dressed as a High Priest, standing in the middle of lampstands that would normally be found just outside the Holy of Holies. We're at the foot of the steps inside the Temple!

John sends seven letters to his seven churches, and each is tailored to the recipient.

- *Revelation 2:1-7.* Ephesus, home of the Temple of Diana (goddess of love) who fell like a meteor from heaven, is warned not to lose their first love.
- *Revelation 2:8-11.* Smyrna that was destroyed and rebuilt is reminded that their suffering will be temporary.
- *Revelation 2:12-17.* Pergamum, center of worship of Caesar, is tackled with a two-edged sword to cut truth from lies and offered manna to replace the pollution of false worship.
- *Revelation 2:18-29* and *Daniel 10:1-6.* The smallest town, Thyatyra, gets the longest message. It was a center for brass working, so Jesus appears as Daniel's bronze-footed statue. They're warned not to dress up false teaching as something better than the truth—a warning the modern world might also need.
- *Revelation 3:1-6.* Sardis, a center for the woolen trade and a city conquered twice while its guards were asleep, is warned that its people are asleep, and promised the gift of white robes.
- *Revelation 3:7-13.* Philadelphia, Gateway to the East, city of loyalty and brotherly love, is praised for its loyalty and called to patience and endurance; they will stand as another gateway—a pillar in the Temple.

- *Revelation 3:14-22.* And finally, rich Laodicea with its aqueduct and lukewarm water, where black woolen garments are made and the medical school is renowned; here they are told to find white clothes and use heavenly eye-salve because they think they are better than they really are. Ouch!

## ENTER THE HOLY OF HOLIES

Having sent his letters, John is invited up the steps into the Holy of Holies where he will find God's throne. Precious stones remind him of the priest's garments. A rainbow reminds him of God's promise and Ezekiel's vision (*Ezekiel 1:28*). Twenty-four elders stand in for the Levitical priesthood, or for twelve tribes and twelve apostles. And thunder roars, as on Mount Sinai long ago. A sea of glass replaces the purification bowl. And four strange creatures (four for the world) echo the creatures in Ezekiel (*Ezekiel 1:5*) and fly like six-winged Seraphim (*Isaiah 6:2*).

A scroll is brought forward, because Temple worship will include the carrying of God's word. But it's sealed, and only the lamb can open the seals.

What follows can be read like a worship service:

1. starting with the carrying of the scroll,
2. then the sounding of trumpets,
3. teaching from the scroll,
4. incense burned on the altar,
5. responses to the Word,
6. rejoicing of the congregation, and
7. finally the Holy of Holies stands open.

Since I love numbers, and seven is a holy number, I enjoy noting there are seven seals, seven trumpets, seven readings, seven bowls, seven descriptions of judgment, seven descriptions of victory and seven visions of the City of God... because that makes seven sevens and what follows must surely be Jubilee (*Leviticus 25:8-13*)! But you don't have to read it that way.

Many interpretations see each repetition in Revelation as a new event. So the earthquake of the sixth seal, the earthquake when incense is thrown down on the earth, another in the time of the witnesses, and another at the seventh trumpet, plus one at the seventh bowl make five earthquakes in all. Reading all the events *sequentially* like this gives a kind of countdown to the end of the world; this feeds appropriate countdown clocks (on the internet perhaps) and helps those who hold this interpretation predict what Jesus himself said we couldn't know. You don't have to read the book that way either.

## (1) CARRYING THE SCROLL

*Revelation 6:1-8:1 describes the seals on the scroll, with a gap between the sixth and seventh, where John sees a vision of "who shall be able to stand."*

The seals, like a contents list to the scroll, describe chapters of disaster; an earthly number (a quarter) die in these pictures—just everyday life. And it starts with four horses, offering images of:

1. conquest,
2. war,
3. famine and
4. death, followed by
5. persecution (still everyday life) and
6. an ending that involves earthquake, falling stars and the sky rolled up... Then
7. silence—"It is finished" perhaps. Like chapter headings in a book, they promise what will be read out during the worship service.

## (2) SOUNDING THE TRUMPETS

*Revelation 8:2-11:19 is where the trumpets sound, calling the world to worship, but first the world is dedicated with incense.*

Seven trumpets call us to worship, starting with four warnings...

1. not to fight God's people with weapons (reminiscent of *Ezekiel 38:22* describing how God defeats the armies at the end of time);
2. not to fight God's people with laws (reminiscent of Jeremiah's prophecy against Babylon in *Jeremiah 51:24-26*);
3. not to think you are better than God (reminding readers of Lucifer's fall in *Isaiah 14:12-15*);
4. and not to think you can keep people away from God (reminding readers of Egypt's plague of darkness in *Exodus 10:21-23*).

Then come three woes, with a brief interlude:

5. God's protection will be withdrawn from the world (with imagery reminiscent of the locusts in *Joel 1:4*. But the trial won't last forever—none of our trials will last forever!).
6. Four angels, perhaps those who've guarded the earth's four corners, leave their posts, setting free the creatures of nightmares (and giving rise to traditional images of demons).
7. Then, after a pause (just like the pause in opening the seals), there's an earthquake. It was promised in the sixth seal / chapter heading, but it isn't even seen as a trial; the curtain of the Temple is gone (*Matthew 27:51*) and the people rejoice.

*Revelation 10 comes between the sixth and seventh trumpets, just as there was a pause before the seventh seal. John is given a message that's both sweet and bitter, and told to keep it secret. Then the Temple is measured, just as in Ezekiel, and two witnesses—maybe representing the law and the prophets—complete their task, just as we shall too. The final trumpet blows and worship begins (Revelation 12:1-15:8).*

## (3) TEACHING FROM THE SCROLL

Worship begins with teaching, or signs, read out from the scroll:

1. A history of salvation—the dragon and the child
2. The deception of false government—the beast from the sea
3. The consequences of false religion—the beast from the earth
4. The union of heaven and earth—and the 144,000
5. God's answer—three angels
6. God's harvest, and
7. A Sabbath rest—vision of the righteous!

## (4) INCENSE BURNED ON THE ALTAR

*Revelation 15:5-16:21 introduces angels carrying bowls of incense, just as priests would in the Temple.*

Not surprisingly, there are seven bowls of incense at this heavenly altar, recalling plagues and passages from the New and Old Testament…

1. the first plague the Egyptian magicians couldn't copy—painful sores caused by those flies;
2. water turning to blood as at the second trumpet's blast;

3. rivers affected too, like the third trumpet's blast, but the angels approve—we approve—because it's all happening according to God's plan, not man's folly;
4. fire, bringing *2 Peter 3:7* to mind—maybe even a fire of purification.
5. The kingdom of the beast is under attack and people curse God. Remembering that Job refused to curse God, where do we put blame and trust?
6. Then, as at the sixth trumpet, the river Euphrates from the Garden of Eden dries up and enemies gather at Armageddon, the hill of Megiddo (*Zechariah 12:11*)
7. And a voice from the Temple cries "It is done"!

## (5) RESPONSES TO THE WORD

*Then it's time for the "sermon" in Revelation 17:1-19:10*

After burning incense the priest would intone God's verdict in the responses. Again, there are seven, describing seven scenes of God's judgment:

1. The whore of Babylon, which may well be *code* for Rome;
2. The angel's explanation;
3. The fall of Babylon;
4. The escape of the saints;
5. A lament over the city;
6. The fate of the city; and finally, in a powerful turnaround,
7. The wedding feast of the Lamb.

Old Testament references abound, as do contemporary ideas, from Babylon reflecting Rome, to seven Roman emperors—Augustus (at Jesus' birth), Tiberius (during Jesus' ministry), Caligula, Claudius (who reigned during the famine in *Acts 11*), Nero (dead and rumored to be planning to rise), Galba and Otho (who both had short reigns).

## (6) REJOICING OF THE CONGREGATION

*Revelation 19:11-20:15 is almost the "final hymn" in this worship service.*

The congregation responds and rejoices in scenes of victory (seven, of course)!

1. A white horse and rider contrasts with the whore on the red beast.
2. The Great Supper, parallels the wedding feast—a victory party announced before the war's even begun!
3. The defeat of the beast and its prophet parallels the fall of Babylon.
4. Satan is bound—in parallel to the escape of the saints.
5. The saints rule—a different view of the lament over the city.
6. Satan is destroyed—not just the city falling. Then
7. the Last Judgment, otherwise known as the Feast of the Lamb.

Of course, people have argued over how long, or when that *millennium* or "thousand years" occurs. For myself, I think it's as symbolic a number as the 144,000—10 (the number for man) raised to the power 3 (for God) gives 1,000. But what matters is the whole thing is under God's power!

## (7) AND THE HOLY OF HOLIES STANDS OPEN

*Revelation 21-22 offers the final answer, and it's all in God's hands!*

The service ends with rejoicing, and visions of the City of God:

1. The New Jerusalem;
2. The Bride of the Lamb;
3. The measuring of the city—a cube like the Holy of Holies;
4. The glory of the city—a new creation as in *Isaiah 60:19*;
5. The water of life—a new river perhaps flowing from heaven instead of Eden;
6. The tree of life restored; and
7. The throne of God.

All that was lost, and more, is restored, and the central theme is not a secret code, but an open message reminding us that God is in control, the end is in His hands, and the future is sure.

Rather than promising that Armageddon will follow the return of the Jews to Jerusalem, or the counting to ten of the European nations, John's message reads, to me anyway, like one of wonder and glory. It's just as my childhood self saw it. However poorly we understand it all, the final ending is the (cubical) Holy of Holies on earth, the priestly jewels on the walls of the city of God, the trees of the Garden of Eden restored, and eternal, wondrous worship.

But let's not try to hurry God along; after all, we'd like all our friends and neighbors and children to know Him first, before He rolls things up.

> *For a fascinating alternative view of Revelation, with a wealth of historical research and detail, read Lee Harmon's* Revelation: The Way it Happened.
>
> *And for a child-friendly journey through Revelation, you could read my own illustrated Easter to Pentecost book:* Revelation! From Easter to Pentecost in 100 words a day.

# Conclusions

**ABOUT FAITH:**

- *Is our faith a misery?* No, it's a joy.
- *Is our faith a pain?* No, it's a healing balm.
- *Is our faith a burden?* No, it lifts burdens and eases distress.
- *Is our faith legalistic?* No, love comes before law.
- *Is our faith divisive?* No, but our people often are.
- *Is our faith cruel?* No, but our people often are.
- *Is our faith a crutch?* No, it's binoculars.
- *Is our faith impractical?* No, but we sometimes make it unworkable.
- *Is our faith a myth?* No, it's rooted in history's realities.
- *Is our faith just part of our culture?* No, it crosses cultural boundaries and expands our horizons.
- *Is our faith unreal?* No, it's the truth behind reality.
- *Is our faith anti-science?* No, it's inextricably bound in reality, which science explores.
- *Is our faith too heavenly minded to be earthly use?* No, but it's sometimes too earthly minded to be used by heaven.
- *Is our faith dying out?* No, because our God has promised He will always be with us to the ending of time.
- *Does our faith predict the end of the world?* No, because even Jesus didn't know.
- *Does our faith tell us who will be saved?* No, but it tells us we will be saved.
- *Does our faith tell us who will be lost?* No, but it warns us against driving anyone away.
- *Does our faith condemn us?* No, but we often condemn ourselves.

- *Does our faith condemn people who aren't like us?* No, it offers comfort and help.
- *Does our faith forgive us?* No, Jesus does that.
- *Is our faith false?* No!

### ABOUT THE BIBLE:

- *Is the Bible scientifically accurate?* It's not a science book, but it doesn't contradict the discoveries of science either.
- *Is the Bible just a bunch of old stories?* No. It's a collection of historical writings, spiritual meditations, archives, poems and more, with a single unifying message, inspired by God.
- *Is the Bible just fairytales about magic?* No. Magicians control their tools to *do* magic. God controls nature and reveals miracles.
- *Is the Bible just a book of "thou shalt nots"?* No, but it contains some amazing rules that kept tribes and nations alive.
- *Is the Bible full of unpleasant war stories?* No, but it contains lots of historical accounts of real wars.
- *Is the Bible cruel?* No, but people often are.
- *Is the Bible useful?* Yes. *Read 2 Timothy 3:16-17* but don't forget, the Scriptures Timothy knew didn't include *2 Timothy!*
- *Is the Bible holy?* Yes!

*If you've read this far, I thank you. And if you'd like to leave a book review, I'd be very grateful.*
*More importantly, if you've read this far,*

**please read your Bible too.**

## AFTERWORD

### Faith is BIG!

Faith gives us a reason to get up when we fall down. It tells us our messed-up lives are worthwhile, and our messed-up world belongs to a perfect God. It says there's a future worth hoping for, and a love that will never betray us.

### Faith is HUGE!

Faith is the greatest gift we can give to our children and grandchildren, and the most wonderful treasure we can share with friends and family… and with strangers. But also…

### Faith is DANGEROUS!

Faith can turn into a rod to beat those strangers' backs—an excuse for us to reject those strangers who can't, don't or won't understand and live the way we believe they should. It turns into a measuring rule, and only those who are just like us will measure up. It turns into a book of impossible commandments. It turns into a millstone instead of a gift, and everyone loses out. Then we lose… faith. And…

### Faith is FREE!

So give it, receive it, share it, read it, delight in it, live in it, freely.